Thailand

by Andrew Forbes & David Henley

Andrew Forbes and David Henley have
both lived in the northern city of Chiang Mai
for more than a decade, together with their
Thai families.

Above: *the warm waters of the Andaman Sea at
Tham Phra Nang Beach, Krabi*

AA Publishing

Above: a long-necked Padaung girl of Mae Hong Son sports traditional brass neck rings

Written by Andrew Forbes and David Henley

Published by AA Publishing, a trading name of Automobile Association Developments Limited, whose registered office is Southwood East, Apollo Rise, Farnborough, Hampshire, GU14 0JW. Registered number 1878835.

© Automobile Association Developments Limited 2001
Reprinted July 2001
Reprinted March 2003
This edition 2005. Information verified and updated.

Maps © 2001 Periplus Editions (HK) Ltd.

Automobile Association Developments Limited retains the copyright in the original edition © 2001 and in all subsequent editions, reprints and amendments.

A CIP catalogue record for this book is available from the British Library.

    The contents of this publication are believed correct at the time of printing. Nevertheless, the publishers cannot be held responsible for any errors or omissions or for changes in the details given in this guide or for the consequences of any reliance on the information it provides. This does not affect your statutory rights. Assessments of attractions, hotels, restaurants and other sights are based upon the author's personal experience and, therefore, necessarily contain elements of subjective opinion which may not reflect the publisher's opinion or dictate a reader's own experience on another occasion.

    We have tried to ensure accuracy in this guide, but things do change and we would be grateful if readers would advise us of any inaccuracies they may encounter.

Find out more about AA Publishing and the wide range of travel publications and services the AA provides by visiting our website at www.theAA.com/bookshop

A01990

Colour separation: Chroma Graphics (Overseas) Pte Ltd, Singapore
Printed and bound in Italy by Printer Trento S.r.l.

Contents

About this Book

KEY TO SYMBOLS

🗺 map reference to the maps found in the What to See section

✉ address or location

☎ telephone number

🕐 opening times

🍴 restaurant or café on premises or nearby

Ⓜ nearest underground train station

🚌 nearest bus/tram route

🚉 nearest overground train station

⛴ ferry crossings and boat excursions

ℹ tourist information

♿ facilities for visitors with disabilities

✋ admission charge

↔ other places of interest nearby

❓ other practical information

▶ indicates the page where you will find a fuller description

✈ travel by air

This book is divided into five sections to cover the most important aspects of your visit to Thailand.

Viewing Thailand pages 5–14
An introduction to Thailand by the authors.
  Thailand's Features
  Essence of Thailand
  The Shaping of Thailand
  Peace and Quiet
  Thailand's Famous

Top Ten pages 15–26
The authors' choice of the Top Ten places to see in Thailand, listed in alphabetical order, each with practical information.

What to See pages 27–90
The four main areas of Thailand, each with its own brief introduction and an alphabetical listing of the main attractions.
  Practical information
  Snippets of 'Did you know…' information
  2 suggested drives
  5 suggested walks
  2 features

Where To... pages 91–116
Detailed listings of the best places to eat, stay, shop, take the children and be entertained.

Practical Matters pages 117–124
A highly visual section containing essential travel information.

Maps
All map references are to the individual maps found in the What to See section of this guide.

For example, Ko Tao has the reference
🗺 54B4 – indicating the page on which the map is located and the grid square in which the island is to be found. A list of the maps that have been used in this travel guide can be found in the index.

Prices
Where appropriate, an indication of the cost of an establishment is given by **£** signs:
£££ denotes higher prices, **££** denotes average prices, while **£** denotes lower charges.

Star Ratings
Most of the places described in this book have been given a separate rating:
❀❀❀   Do not miss
❀❀   Highly recommended
❀   Worth seeing

Viewing
Thailand

Above: *floating market at Thonburi,
Bangkok*
Right: *detail of fruit carving*

The Authors' Thailand

Land of the Free
Through a fortuitous mixture of good luck (Great Britain and France were more interested in keeping each other out than in taking over) and the far-sighted modernising philosophies espoused by King Mongkut (1851–68) and King Chulalongkorn (1868–1910), Siam, as Thailand was then known, remained independent throughout the colonial period. Perhaps because of this, Thai people are particularly welcoming and courteous to foreigners. They are very open to new ideas and fashions; if they like something, they will embrace it with open arms. Yet they remain distinctively Thai, with a confidence in their unique cultural identity.

Thailand is a fortunate land. Literally translated, its name can mean 'Land of the Free', and indeed – almost alone in Asia – it escaped colonisation by the West. Fertile, warm and washed by the seas of two oceans (the Indian and the Pacific), the country can easily feed its rapidly stabilising population with plenty left over for export. Its people are friendly, hence the popular epithet 'Land of Smiles', and the scenery, from the mountainous north to the jewel-like islands and pristine beaches of the south, is of great beauty.

This tropical paradise also boasts a cuisine that is delicious, varied and features a mouth-watering selection of familiar and exotic fruits. Not surprisingly, tourism has become a major industry, encouraging over the past 25 years the development of the most sophisticated and diverse destination in the region. Getting to Thailand is increasingly easy and reasonably priced, and the range of accommodation is unsurpassed, from sumptuous international resorts and luxury hotels to clean and comfortable guest houses.

Thailand is not just a delight for hedonists seeking a suntan. This ancient kingdom has produced some of the most outstanding architecture in the world. From the Grand Palace in the national capital, Bangkok, to the temple-studded city of Chiang Mai in the north, a plethora of attractions awaits the visitor. Saffron-clad Buddhist monks, colourful minority hill tribes and the general population bear daily witness to Thailand's age-old culture and traditions. They form a vibrant backdrop for adventurous pursuits such as elephant riding, trekking, rafting and scuba-diving. An internationally renowned nightlife and world-class shopping ensure this destination satisfies every taste and purpose.

Patong Beach, on Phuket island

Thailand's Features

Lisu women threshing grain in the hills near Pai

Geography

Thailand has an area of 513,998sq km or 198,455sq miles. It is generally divided geographically into four areas: the mountainous north, the vast arid plateau of the northeast, the flat central plains dominated by Bangkok, and the peninsular south, famous for its beaches and islands. Bangkok's population fluctuates around 10 million, depending on the time of year, as migrants from rural areas seek off-season work. The capital is more than 40 times larger than any other Thai city and dominates much of the nation's economic, political and cultural life.

Climate

Thailand's weather can be divided broadly into three seasons – hot, when the temperature soars to around 35°C everywhere and Bangkok really swelters; rainy, when the southwest monsoon brings life-giving rain and the temperature is over 30°C; and cool, when it is around 29°C during the day and can be quite chilly at night. The timing of these seasons varies across the country. In Bangkok the hot season runs from around March to April, the rainy season from May to October and the cool season from November to February.

People

Thailand is an ethnically homogeneous country. Thai (and closely related Lao) people make up more than 75 per cent of the country's 62 million inhabitants. The remainder of the population includes a well-integrated ethnic Chinese minority (about 11 per cent), Malay-speaking Muslims in the deep south (5 per cent), roughly two million native Cambodian speakers in the northeast, and members of perhaps a dozen hill tribes in the north and west, especially Karen, Lisu, Lahu, Akha, Hmong and Yao.

Thai Names

Thai names often seem long to foreigners and even to Thais themselves, who tend to use short nicknames. The simplest correct form of address, regardless of sex, is to add the prefix 'Khun'. Thais have a given or first name and a family or second name. They are never addressed by the family name but always by their given name or nickname. Thus, Puangphet Jinagan, nicknamed 'Maew' ('cat' in Thai) would be addressed as Khun Puangphet or Khun Maew.

7

Essence of Thailand

Above: *monks gathering at Wat Arun, Thonburi, in central Bangkok*

Right: *lotus pond set in a fertile northern valley*

Nation, religion and monarchy – in Thai, *chat, sat* and *pramahakasat* – are the cornerstones of life and are apparent from the moment your plane touches down.

The Thais love their country with a passion that is mellow and heartfelt, never strident or aggressive. They invariably stand when the national anthem is played – as in cinemas – and foreigners are expected to follow suit. They show a similar love for the royal family (especially the king), whose pictures hang in every house and business.

The influence of Theravada Buddhism is also pervasive. From the heart of Bangkok to remote country villages, soft chanting in Pali by saffron-clad monks and temple bells fill the air. Practising Buddhist Thais hate to kill anything and the stray dog population is a major beneficiary of this benevolence. Thais also like to eat meat, though; a dilemma easily solved by the country's three million Muslims, many of whom work in the butchery business.

In a country renowned for its wild nightlife, the Thais can be extremely modest; revealing clothing is considered impolite and nude sunbathing or swimming quite unacceptable. Combine this with an astonishing liberality of attitude – gays and transvestites are readily accepted – and you have the beginnings of the charming enigma that is the essence of Thailand.

THE **10** ESSENTIALS

*If you only have a short time to visit Thailand,
or would like to get a complete picture of
the country, here are the essentials:*

- **Visit the Grand Palace**
The gilded Grand Palace
(▶ 18–19) and associated
temples and museums on
Ratanakosin Island, in the
heart of Bangkok, are literally
dazzling.
- **See Jim Thompson's
House**
On a sleepy backstreet of
downtown Bangkok, this
delightful amalgamation of
traditional Thai wooden
buildings houses an
exquisite collection of
priceless Thai, Burmese and
Cambodian antiquities
(▶ 36).

- **Visit a tropical island**
Setting for the Leonardo
DiCaprio film *The Beach,*
Thailand has hundreds of the
most pristine tropical islands
in the world. Choose Phuket
(▶ 57), Ko Samui (▶ 62) or
a less well-developed island
such as Ko Chang (▶ 50).
- **See a hill-tribe village**
Trek into the hills of north
Thailand on foot or by
elephant and spend a night
or two with the hospitable,
brightly dressed minority
peoples of the area.
- **View a Khmer temple**
Go to Phanom Rung (▶ 23)
or Phimai (▶ 90) – better
yet, visit both. These are the
world's best-preserved
Khmer temples dating from
the classical Angkor period.
- **Go to Chiang Mai**
The legendary 'Rose of the
North', nestling in the lee of
Doi Suthep, is a 700-year-old
walled and moated city with
a well-deserved reputation
for hospitality and more than
100 temples (▶ 68).
- **Taste Thai food**
Thailand has one of the
greatest culinary traditions in
the world. The cuisine is not

always hot but it is, nearly
always, refined and
delicious. It is also generally
healthy and non-fattening.
- **Visit a Buddhist temple**
A visit to a Thai temple, or
wat, where serene monks sit
chanting age-old Pali
scriptures, is an essential
ingredient to understanding
the country.
- **See some traditional
dancing**
Classical Thai dance, rooted
in the traditions of classical
India, is exquisitely
sophisticated. One of the
best places to see a
performance is at
Bangkok's Erawan
Shrine (▶ 36).
- **Explore a Thai
market**
Almost any
market will do,
but for a real
experience go
to one of
the 'floating
markets' by
boat early
in the
morning when
trading is at its
peak (▶ 44).

*Batik cloth for sale in a
Phuket souvenir shop*

*Chillies, garlic and other
ingredients are used to
make spicy Si
Racha Pepper
Sauce*

The Shaping of Thailand

4000 BC
A pottery-producing society is established at Ban Chiang in Khon Kaen province (north-eastern Thailand).

AD 100
Mon culture of Dvaravati develops in the Chao Phraya Valley. Traders and Theravada Buddhist missionaries introduce Indic culture.

400–1000
Eastern and central Thailand form part of the Khmer Empire. Thai-speaking peoples gradually migrate south from China into present-day Thailand.

1238
The first independent Thai Kingdom is founded at Sukhothai (northern Thailand), marking the start of a golden age.

1279–98
King Ramkhamhaeng of Sukhothai develops the Thai script and extends Thai control to present-day peninsular Thailand.

1296
King Mengrai establishes Chiang Mai as capital of the second independent Thai Kingdom of Lan Na.

1351
Siamese power moves to the central plains

with the founding of the Ayuthaya Kingdom north of present-day Bangkok.

1432
Ayuthaya sacks Angkor, supplanting the Khmer Empire as the major regional power.

1511
Portugal establishes the first European embassy in Ayuthaya.

1549
Burma begins a series of destructive attacks on Ayuthaya, eventually

The impressive statue of King Narai (1657–1688) who was responsible for reviving and restoring the city of Lopburi

succeeding in over-running the country.

1558
Burma conquers Chiang Mai and makes the former Lan Na Kingdom its tributary.

1587
King Naresuan drives out the Burmese.

1657–88
King Narai establishes diplomatic relations with several European powers.

1767
Ayuthaya is invaded and burned by the Burmese. General Taksin reorganises the Siamese armies and drives out the invaders. He becomes king and transfers the capital to Thonburi, on the west bank of the Chao Phraya River opposite the small settlement of Bangkok.

1782
King Taksin, accused of madness, is toppled by his leading general, Chao Phraya Chakri, and put to death. The new ruler proclaims himself King Rama I, founder of the Chakri Dynasty that is still in place today. He moves his capital to Bangkok, which he renames Krungthep ('City of Angels').

1851–68
King Mongkut (Rama IV), a well-educated and far-sighted reformer, signs a friendship treaty with Great Britain and begins a modernisation process that will eventually protect his country from colonisation.

1868–1910
King Chulalongkorn (Rama V) advances his father's policies, instituting wide-ranging reforms and leading an independent Siam into the 20th century.

1917
Siam enters World War 1 as an ally of the victorious powers.

1932
A military coup ends the absolute powers of the king. Siam becomes a constitutional monarchy.

1935
Ten-year-old Ananda Mahidol becomes King Rama VIII.

1939
Military strongman Pibul Songkhram becomes Prime Minister. Siam changes its name to Thailand.

1939–45
During World War II Thailand becomes an ally of Japan. After the

A fine bronze statue of King Rama VIII catches the light in an archway in Wat Suthat

war, Britain initially seeks to punish the country, but the United States steps in as Thailand's main ally.

1945–73
Thailand remains a firm ally of the West in the Cold War, but is plagued by military coups.

1946
King Mahidol dies. His younger brother, Bhumibol Adulyadej, accedes to the throne and is crowned King Rama IX in 1950.

1973
Student demonstrators are involved in street battles with soldiers, resulting in almost 70 deaths. The military

government is forced to resign, but, despite a new constitution, the army retains real power.

1976–92
Thailand achieves major economic advances but remains essentially autocratic. Tourism begins to thrive.

1992
General Suchinda comes to power, following an army coup the previous year. Resulting protests lead to the deaths of more than 50 demonstrators and Suchinda's resignation. Democracy is established and Chuan Leekpai becomes Prime Minister.

1997
Asia's economic collapse weakens Thailand's 'tiger economy' status.

2000
King Bhumibol is revered at home. Thailand's economy and democratic institutions are strengthening.

2001
Thaksin Shinawatra, Thailand's wealthiest entrepreneur, becomes prime minister.

11

Peace & Quiet

Most visitors arrive in Thailand by way of Don Muang, Bangkok's hectic airport and one of the major transport hubs for the region. They then enter the city via an elevated series of toll roads passing through and over a vast megalopolis with a population of around 10 million people. Under these circumstances it is hard to believe that Thailand has many unrivalled opportunities to escape modern life's stresses.

Idyllic view across a turquoise sea

Nature lovers, however, can enjoy 79 national parks, 89 wildlife sanctuaries and 35 forest reserves. Some of these unspoilt regions lie surprisingly close to Bangkok, including Khao Yai, Thailand's first national park, which covers 2,200sq km and includes one of the largest tropical monsoon forests on the Asian mainland. More than 50km of hiking trails offer access to wild elephants, sambar deer, Malayan sun bears, Asiatic black bears and a wealth of bird life. There are even some surviving tigers and leopards.

A tiger takes a cooling dip in a lotus pond

Also close to Bangkok is the river resort town of Kanchanaburi, best known as the site of the infamous bridge over the River Kwai. Kanchanaburi is an ideal place to relax in a private houseboat, although floating discos can make it noisy at night. You can also hike to see spectacular nearby waterfalls and eat at the town's excellent restaurants.

Further afield, the north is famous for hill-tribe trekking, while the Gulf of Siam and Andaman Sea are dotted with many almost deserted islands. In contrast to well-developed resort islands such as Phuket and Ko Samui, ones such as Ko Chang, near the Cambodian border, retain a pristine, Robinson Crusoe atmosphere and are still inexpensive to visit.

Thailand has seven marine national parks where an extensive variety of sea creatures may be observed by kayak, glass-bottomed boat, snorkelling and diving. Thousand-year-old hilltop Khmer temples, the banks of the Mekong River and the summit of Thailand's tallest mountain, Doi Inthanon, are also peaceful stopping places.

More than twice the size of the United Kingdom with about the same population, Thailand is still predominantly rural – with a correspondingly laid-back atmosphere – outside Bangkok.

Tropical butterflies sipping dew at a national park in the south

A view across Khao Sok National Park

Thailand's Famous

King Bhumibol Adulyadej (r1946–)
Thailand's king and currently the longest reigning monarch in the world was born in Boston, Massachusetts, and educated partly in the United States and Switzerland. King Bhumibol returned to Thailand after World War II to find the monarchy in a position of relative weakness. Since then he has restored the power of the constitutional monarchy, the role of democracy in his country, and respect and love for the royal family.

King Chulalongkorn (Rama V)

Chang and Eng (c1811–74)
The celebrated first-reported conjoined twins (hence the term 'Siamese twins') were discovered in Bangkok in 1824. Chang and Eng migrated to America where they both married, raised extensive families and finally died within hours of each other.

King Chulalongkorn (r1868–1910)
The fifth monarch of the reigning Chakri Dynasty and Siam's most venerated king, Chulalongkorn is widely credited with preserving Siam's freedom at a time of rampant Western colonialism. He introduced sweeping political and social reforms, setting Siam on the road to development and independence as a modern nation state.

Khaosai Galaxy (1959–)
Thailand's most celebrated and popular boxer successfully defended the 115-pound world title 19 times. At the height of his career, he was the best pound-for-pound boxer in the world, and this in a period when Mike Tyson was the undisputed heavyweight champion.

Anand Panyarachun (1932–)
Credited with helping restore democracy following the 1991 military coup, Anand was Thailand's Prime Minister from 1991–92. A graduate of Trinity College, Cambridge (UK), he was ambassador to the United States in 1972 and deputy foreign minister in 1976.

Kukrit Pramoj (1911–95)
Intellectual, novelist and political columnist, Kukrit was Prime Minister of Thailand (1975–76) and became a respected elder statesman. He acted opposite Marlon Brando in the 1963 film *The Ugly American* in which he played the Prime Minister of a Southeast Asian nation.

Porntip Nakhirunkanok (1968–)
Thais are passionate about beauty contests and Porntip, Miss Universe 1988, is considered the most successful Miss Thailand. The television announcer with a master's degree in psychology also works for children's charities.

Tiger Woods (1975–)
American golfer Tiger Woods, whose mother is Thai, has been claimed by Thais as one of their own. One of the greatest golfers in the world today, he has been granted Thai citizenship, although he has never lived in the country.

Top Ten

Above: *mural depicting the Ramakien in Wat Phra Kaeo at the Grand Palace*
Right: *gilded temple guardian at Wat Phra Kaeo*

1
Chatuchak
Weekend Market

*Roses at Chatuchak
Weekend Market*

*Almost 9,000 stalls cater to an estimated 200,000
daily visitors at the king of Thai markets.*

 Off map

 Southern end of
Chatuchak Park, off
Thanon Phahon Yothin,
Bangkok

 Sat–Sun 8–6

 Cafés in all sections of
the market

N8, Mor Chit Station

2, 3, 9, 10, 13

 Few

 Free

Musical events in the
late afternoon

From endangered wildlife to opium pipes, hill-tribe crafts
to herbal remedies, everything is sold at Bangkok's
weekend market. Musical instruments, religious amulets,
antiques, flowers, clothes imported from India and Nepal,
camping gear and military surplus equipment are regular
items. The best bargains are household goods
such as pots and pans, dishes, drinking glasses and
second-hand books.

You might feel overwhelmed by the scale of the
market, the bustling crowds and the heat, but take
time to wander because this is the ideal place to buy
Thai handicrafts or souvenirs. Be sure to bargain
good-naturedly, pitching your initial offer at least 50 per
cent below the asking price.

One unfortunate aspect of the market is the sale of
some endangered wildlife, both living (as pets) and dead
(for medicine or the cooking pot). Recently the Thai
authorities have moved to crack down on this illicit trade,
which is far less prevalent than a decade ago.

Plenty of interesting and tasty food and drink stalls,
and live music towards the end of the day, complete
the recommended full-day visit. Although the market
is mainly open at the weekend, a few vendors are out
on weekday mornings and there is a daily vegetable,
plant and flower market opposite the weekend market's
south side.

2
Doi Inthanon

*Thailand's highest peak hosts a unique ecosystem
of sub-Himalayan flora and fauna.*

Encompassed in a 428sq km national park, the 2,595m-high Doi Inthanon was named after Phra Inthawichayanon, the last king of Chiang Mai, who died at the turn of the 19th century. His remains lie interred in a small white *chedi* (pagoda) near the summit. Long celebrated by the people of the north for its natural beauty and cool climate, the mountain has much to offer, including unspoilt hill-tribe villages, four striking waterfalls and dramatic mountain scenery.

Once the habitat of bears and tigers, the park has seen the severe depletion of its wildlife by overhunting and increased human settlement. Nevertheless, it is still possible to see rare mammals such as flying squirrels, red-toothed shrews, Chinese pangolins and Père David's vole, as well as a plethora of birds, butterflies and moths. Rainfall on the slopes is high, with frequent showers even during the dry season. This encourages myriad varieties of ferns, mosses and orchids to flourish, often completely covering the trunks of even the tallest trees.

Nearer the summit stand two tall pagodas built to honour the Thai king and queen. These remarkable structures, set amid carefully tended gardens of temperate flowers and vegetables, are among the most architecturally innovative buildings of their kind in Thailand. Particularly noteworthy are the modernistic interpretations of traditional Buddhist themes portrayed in copper-coloured tiles on the face of the king's *stupa*. In borders nearby, fuchsias, petunias, hydrangeas, helicrishams and salvias blend unexpectedly with decorative cabbages, adding to the location's charm.

✚ 74A3

✉ 113km southwest of Chiang Mai

🕐 Daily

🍴 Café next to royal *chedis* (pagodas)

🚌 Buses from Chiang Mai to Chom Thong, then *songthaews* to summit

ℹ Chiang Mai–Lamphun Road, Chiang Mai
☎ (053) 248604

♿ None

✋ Cheap

Queen's stupa, the summit of Doi Inthanon

3
Grand Palace

Prepare to be dazzled by the wealth of cultural and architectural delights that await visitors here.

The greatest site in Bangkok and a definite 'must' on any itinerary is the Grand Palace and the surrounding monuments on Ko Ratanakosin (Ratanakosin Island ➤ 39). The main attraction at the palace itself – which is only used by the monarch on certain ceremonial occasions, his official residence in Bangkok being Dusit Palace – is Wat Phra Kaeo, the 'Temple of the Emerald Buddha'. This tiny but elegant Buddha image, made of jasper and only 75cm high, stands at the heart of the temple on a high

Top: *a temple guard statue with an image of Buddha built into his helmet*
Above: *gilded Buddha image revered by worshippers, Wat Phra Kaeo*

Resting in the shade of a sala (open-sided pavilion) beside Wat Phra Kaeo

18

✚ 34A3

✉ Thanon Sanam Chai

☎ (02) 623 5499

🕐 Daily 8:30–3:30

🚌 8, 12

♿ Good

✋ Moderate

pedestal encased in glass. Regarded as the Palladium of the Kingdom, it cannot be photographed and – perhaps partly because of this – it is surrounded by a palpable aura of mystery and respect.

Top: *a statue with blue painted face supports part of the building at Wat Phra Kaeo*
Above: *a woman making a floral offering*

4
Khao Sok National Park

 54A3

 Off Route 401, 100km north of Phuket

Daily

Restaurants at resorts just outside the park

Bus from Phuket to Takua Pa, bus from Takua Pa to Surat Thani, get off at KM 109

None

Cheap

A butterfly with pale yellow and black markings, perched on a white flower

This 650sq km park in Surat Thani, southern Thailand, boasts original rainforest with water-falls, limestone cliffs and an island-studded lake.

Established in 1980, Khao Sok connects with two other national parks, Kaeng Krung and Phang-nga, along with the Khlong Saen and Khlong Nakha wildlife sanctuaries. Together, they form the largest contiguous nature preserve in peninsular Thailand.

Home to elephants, leopards, serow (antelope), gaur (wild Indian cattle), langur monkeys, banteng (wild oxen) and Malayan sun bears, as well as almost 200 bird species, the park also shelters tigers, seriously threatened elsewhere in Thailand by poachers (the Khao Sok tiger population itself is thought to number less than 10).

Flora includes lianas, bamboo, rattan, ferns and the spectacular *Raffelesia*, the giant lotus – its flower reaches 80cm in diameter and is the largest in the world. The flower has no roots or leaves of its own; instead it lives parasitically inside the roots of the liana. When the bud blooms in January it emits a powerful stench which attracts pollinating insects.

The best time of year to visit Khao Sok is in the dry season (December to May), when trails are less slippery, river crossings are easier and riverbank camping is considered safe. However, during the wet season, sightings of larger animals such as bear, civet, deer, elephant, slow loris, wild boar, gaur and even tiger are more likely. During dry months the larger animals tend to stay near the reservoir in areas without trails.

The park headquarters and guest houses near the park entrance can arrange guided hikes to the main waterfalls and caves. Leeches are quite common in certain areas of the park, so take sensible precautions – wear closed shoes when hiking and apply copious insect repellent.

5
Mekong River

One of the world's great waterways, the Mekong flows for more than 4,500km – a third of which it spends dallying between Thailand and Laos.

Until recently the Mekong formed part of the 'bamboo curtain' between communist and non-communist Asia. It is now fast becoming a gateway to Laos and Cambodia, as well as a fascinating crossroads for Indo-Chinese culture.

Rising in a distant region of China, the Mekong passes through six countries before emptying into the South China Sea. For 1,500km of this course, the mighty river flows partly in Thai territory, first appearing at Sop Ruak in the far north and forming the border between Thailand and Laos as far as Chiang Kham (town of the giant Mekong catfish or *plaa beuk*) before cutting back into Laos. It reappears in Thailand near Chiang Khan in Isaan, Thailand's northeastern region, and again forms the Thai-Lao border in a great arc, finally disappearing into Laos just beyond Khong Jiam on its way to the thunderous Khone Falls.

The Mekong is Isaan's lifeline, a constant source of water. As a consequence, the riverside settlements which border it from Chiang Khan in the north to Mukdahan and beyond in the east are the most favoured parts of Isaan – and the most interesting towns to visit.

The Mekong can be experienced in the north at Chiang Saen and the Golden Triangle (► 76), or during the long and relaxing drive from Chiang Khan to Nong Khai and even on to Mukdahan (► 89).

75C5–D2, 84–85A4–D1

The border in north and northeast Thailand

Restaurants the complete length

Regular air-conditioned buses to all major towns on the river from Bangkok

Train to Nong Khai

Boats from Chiang Saen to Sop Ruak

Sunset over the Mekong River, off the coast of Chiang Mai

6
Phang-nga Bay

 54A3

✉ Phang-nga Bay,
788km south of
Bangkok, 95km
north of Phuket

🚌 Regular air-conditioned
buses from Bangkok
and Phuket

⛴ Boat trips into Phang-
nga Bay from Tha Dan

✖ Phuket Airport

ℹ Phuket TAT Office,
Phuket Road
☎ (076) 211036

♿ None

✋ Moderate
Sea Canoe Thailand
☎ (076) 212172

*The limestone formation
of Ko Tapu, Phang-nga
Bay, setting for the
The Man With the
Golden Gun*

*Several companies based in Phuket offer boat tours
of scenic Phang-nga Bay.*

About 95km from Phuket, the area around Phang-nga Bay
is startlingly beautiful – sheer limestone cliffs ring the bay,
while unlikely karst towers carved over the millennia into
extraordinary shapes rise sheer from the azure waters. It is
one of the scenic wonders of the world.

The bay can be explored aboard large boats on
organised tours, or individually chartered 'long-tail' boats
that are fast but noisy. Nothing beats kayaking in the
region, however. The inflatable kayaks or canoes can enter
semi-submerged caves inaccessible to larger boats,
sometimes passing beneath overhangs so low that the
canoeist has to lie flat.

Absolute silence reigns within these sea caves, save for
the dripping of water from a nearby stalactite or the splash
of a paddle. One visitor noted that he was startled by the
beating of a butterfly's wings. The caves often open into
large hidden bowls, inaccessible from the top, which fill
with sunlight during the day and are home to interesting
flora and fauna, including flocks of swallows, the nests of
which are used to make bird's-nest soup.

Other sights to look for when exploring Phang-nga Bay
are 'James Bond Island', a narrow island tower made
famous in the 007 movie *The Man With the Golden Gun*,
and the Muslim fishing village on Panyi Island.

7

Prasat Phanom Rung

Built between the 10th and 13th centuries, Prasat Phanom Rung is the largest and best preserved Khmer monument outside Cambodia.

The architecture of the kingdom of Angkor reached its apogee during the reign of King Suriyavarman II (AD 1113–50), when the greater part of the work on Prasat Phanom Rung was completed.

Phanom Rung was originally built as a Hindu temple honouring the deities Vishnu and Shiva. Beautifully carved representations of these two gods adorn the lintels and pediments of the sanctuary, together with figures of Nandi, the bull mount of Shiva and Uma. On the east portico of the antechamber is a fine *nataraja* or dancing Shiva figure. Beyond, in the rust-coloured central section of the sanctuary, is a Shiva *lingam* (phallic image).

The famed Phra Narai lintel, a carved relief bearing the image of Lord Narayana (a manifestation of Vishnu), is over the east-facing front entrance. Growing from his navel is a lotus blossom, on a branch of which sits Brahma, the Hindu lord of creation.

One of the most impressive sights of the sanctuary is from the west-facing laterite promenade that leads straight to the main temple. In the early morning the rising sun illuminates the steps and *naga* (mythical Hindu water serpent) balustrades leading to the inner complex containing the central *mondop* (ante-chamber) and main *prang* (spire). The promenade passes the White Elephant Hall on the right.

The climb to the sanctuary from the car park is gradual and passes a number of small museum buildings housing artefacts from the site, including carved stone lintels. It took 20 years to restore the sanctuary.

✚ 28C4

✉ 144km southeast of Nakhon Ratchasima

🕐 Daily 6–6

🍴 Food stalls at entrance

🚌 Regular buses from Nakhon Ratchasima, Buriram and Surin

ℹ Mittaphap Road, Nakhon Ratchasima
☎ (044) 213666

♿ None   **✋** Cheap

❓ Phanom Rung Festival, Mar

The central tower of Prasat Phanom Rung dates from the 12th century

8
Similan Islands

 29A2

📧 100km northwest of Phuket

🕐 All year round

🍽 Restaurant on Ko Miang

⛴ Regular tour boats from Phuket

ℹ TAT Office, Phuket Road, Phuket Town ☎ (076) 212213

♿ None

💰 Cheap

View of one of the Similan Islands

The Similans are renowned for their rich coral reefs, clear waters and pristine beaches.

These islands are a naturalist's paradise. Marine animals include whale sharks, manta rays, bottlenose dolphins and large pelagic fish, along with interesting smaller life from garden eels to feather stars. More than 30 species of resident birds, such as the white-breasted waterhen and Brahminy kite, and migratory species, including the cattle egret, pintail snipe, grey wagtail and roseate tern, occupy the islands. Small mammals include the bush-tailed porcupine, common palm civet and flying lemur. Reptiles and amphibians include the banded krait, reticulated python, white-lipped pit viper, common pit viper, hawksbill turtle, leatherback turtle, Bengal monitor lizard and common water monitor lizard.

The name 'Similan' derives from the Malay word *sembilan* or nine and refers to the nine islands in the group. All are relatively small and uninhabited except for park officials and tour groups.

Divers generally prefer visiting the Similans on one of the many live-aboard boats that operate out of Phuket. Other visitors stay on Ko Miang, second in size to Ko Similan, where there is a visitors' centre, the park headquarters and the archipelago's only land accommodation. The beaches on this island are especially good for shallow-water snorkelling. Nearby Ko Similan is popular for walking and snorkelling. The largest granite outcrop in the archipelago is also found on Ko Similan and from the top there is a fine view of the surrounding sea.

Boats run to the Similans between November and May only, with the best diving months between December and May. For the remainder of the year the seas are too rough and water visibility is reduced.

9
Sukhothai Historical Park

The remains of 21 structures lie within the old walls of the capital of the first Thai kingdom, once fortified by three ramparts and two moats.

Ramkhamhaeng National Museum provides a good starting point for an exploration of the ruins. A replica of the famous Ramkhamhaeng inscription – the earliest known example of Thai script, dating from the reign of King Ramkhamhaeng of Sukhothai (1279–98) – is on show, together with a fine collection of Sukhothai artefacts.

Sukhothai temple architecture is typified by the classic lotus-bud *stupa*, which features a conical spire topping a square-sided structure on a three-tiered base. Some sites also exhibit other rich architectural forms introduced and modified during the period (1240–96), such as bell-shaped Sinhalese and double-tiered Srivijaya *stupas*.

The spiritual and administrative centre of the old capital, Wat Mahathat is the largest temple in the city and dates from the 13th century. Surrounded by brick walls and a moat, the *stupa* exhibits the lotus-bud motif while almost 200 original Buddha images survive among the ruined columns. Just to the south, the 12th-century Wat Si Sawai, originally a Hindu temple, features three Khmer-style *prangs* (spires) and a picturesque moat.

Next to the museum, Wat Trapang Thong is a small, still functioning temple with fine stucco reliefs. It is reached by a footbridge across the large lotus-filled pond surrounding it. This tank, which still supplies the Sukhothai community with most of its water, is supposedly the original site of Thailand's Loy Krathong Festival (when lighted candles are set adrift on rivers and canals in honour of Mae Kongka, goddess of the waterways).

The elephant, an animal traditionally held in great esteem by the Thais, features prominently at Sukhothai. Wat Chang Lom (Elephant Circled Monastery) is about a kilometre east of the main park entrance. A large bell-shaped *chedi* (pagoda) is supported by 36 elephants sculpted into its base. On another hill west of the city, just south of Wat Saphaan Hin, Wat Chang Rop also features an elephant-base *stupa*.

75C1

✉ Old Sukhothai, 12km from New Sukhothai; 400km north of Bangkok

🕐 Daily 6–6

🍴 Food stalls within the park

🚌 Regular *songthaews* (pick-up vans converted to buses) from New Sukhothai

✈ Sukhothai Airport

ℹ Sukhothai Travel Service ☎ (055) 613075

♿ Few

✋ Moderate

❓ Loy Krathong Festival, Nov

Sunset over Wat Mahathat

10
Wat Phra That Lampang Luang

74B3

18km southwest of Lampang city (which is 90km southeast of Chiang Mai), Ko Kha district, north Thailand

Daily 6–6

Food stalls outside temple complex

Regular *songthaews* from Lampang

Lampang Station

Lampang Airport

None

Free

Right: *Wat Phra That Lampang Luang*

Below: *gilt painting of thevadas (angels) at Wat Phra That Lampang Luang*

Believed to contain a genuine Buddha relic, northern Thailand's most beautiful temple is revered by the Thai people.

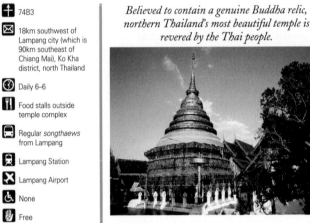

Established in Mon times, during the Kingdom of Haripunchai, Wat Phra That Lampang Luang (the 'Great Temple of Lampang') is in Ko Kha district, 18km southwest of the city of Lampang. It was originally a *wiang* or fortified temple protected by massive earthen ramparts. The tall central *chedi* (pagoda) is believed to contain a bone fragment of the Buddha and is widely revered by Thai people, especially the Khon Muang (northern Thais).

On important religious holidays, notably at Songkran (Thai New Year) and Loy Krathong (Festival of Lights) each November full moon, the temple attracts huge crowds of devout worshippers from Lampang and more distant provinces. Particularly venerated is the Phra Kaeo Don Tao, a jasper Buddha image believed to have mystical powers.

In architectural terms, Wat Phra That Lampang Luang is one of Thailand's most elegant temples. The central *viharn* (chapel), featuring a triple-tiered wooden roof supported by massive teak pillars, is thought to be the oldest wooden building in Thailand. Early 19th-century murals from the Buddhist *jatakas* or life stories are painted on wooden panels within the *viharn*. The lintel (horizontal support) over the main entrance to the compound has an impressive intertwined dragon relief – once common in northern Thai temples but rarely seen today.

What To See

Above: *kites for sale at Sanam Luang, Bangkok*
Right: *a small girl carrying a parasol in Chiang Mai*

27

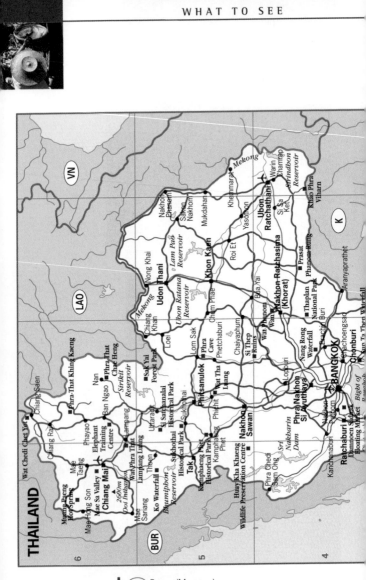

BUR Burma (Myanmar)

LAO Laos

VN Vietnam

K Cambodia

MAL Malaysia

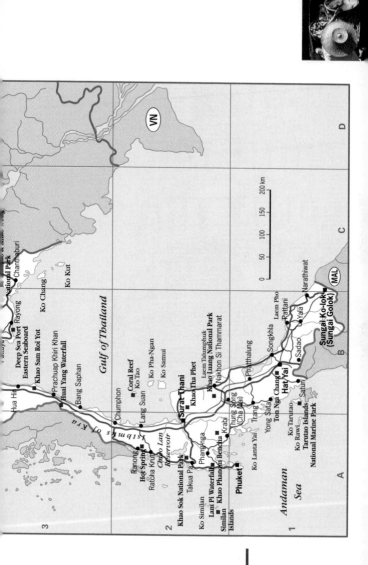

VN

Chanthaburi
National Park
Ko Kut

Ko Chang

Rayong
Deep Sea Port
Eastern Seaboard
Khao Sam Roi Yot
Prachuap Khiri Khan
Huai Yang Waterfall

Gulf of Thailand

Bang Saphan

Hua Hin

Coral Reef
Ko Tao
Ko Pha-Ngan
Ko Samui

Chumphon
Lang Suan

Laem Pho
Pattani
Narathiwat
Yala
Songkhla

Isthmus of Kra

Surat Thani
Khao Tha Phet
Laem Talumphuk
Khao Luang National Park
Nakhon Si Thammarat

Phatthalung
Ton Nga Chang
Hat Yai
Sadao
Satun

MAL

Sungai Ko-lok
(Sungai Golok)

Ranong
Hot Spring
Ratcha Krut
*Chiao Lan
Reservoir*
Takua Pa
Phang-nga
Krabi

Khao Sok National Park

Ko Similan
Lam Pi Waterfall
Khao Phanom Bencha
Similan
Islands
Phuket

Thung Song
(Cha Mai)
Trang
Yong Safa
Ko Lanta Yai

Ko Tarutao
Ko Rawi
Tarutao Islands
National Marine Park

*Andaman
Sea*

| 0 | 50 | 100 | 150 | 200 km |

3

2

1

A   B   C   D

Central Thailand

The broad, fertile plains of Central Thailand form the traditional heartland of old Siam, as they have since the Thai capital moved south from Sukhothai to Ayuthaya in the mid-14th century. Central Thailand, dominated by Bangkok, is the political powerhouse of the country. It provides the national language – Thai – which is spoken throughout the kingdom and understood everywhere, even by those whose first language is a regional dialect (such as the Northern Thai people) or a distinct minority language (as in the hill tribes).

Although perhaps the least scenically attractive region of Thailand, the central plains feature not only Bangkok but the ancient royal cities of Ayuthaya and Lopburi, where fascinating ruins reflect the country's past. Kanchanaburi, in the west, is a charming rural idyll just a couple of hours from the bustle of the capital; then there are the delightful floating markets, most notably at Damnoen Saduak.

'To Bangkok! Magic name, blessed name'

JOSEPH CONRAD,
Youth (1898)

———————●———————

Left: *Khmer-style* prang at Wat Ratchaburana, Ayuthaya

Two views of Bangkok, Thailand's bustling modern metropolis

Bangkok

When Siam's King Rama I established his new capital on a bend in the Chao Phraya River in 1782, he chose an easily defensible site where an old fort, called Bang Makok, or Bangkok for short, already existed. This name, although of venerable age, means 'place of olive plums', and was deemed insufficiently noble for a royal city. Accordingly, when the capital was first consecrated, it was given a new title which is still the longest place name in the world:

Krungthepmahanakhonbowonrattanakos-inmahintaraayutthayamahadilokpopnopparatratch-athaniburiromudomratchaniwetmahasathanamon-pimanavatansathirsakkathatityavisnukamprasit.

In English, this may be rendered: 'Great City of Angels, City of Immortals, Magnificent Jewelled City of the God Indra, Seat of the King of Ayutthaya, City of Gleaming Temples, City of the King's Most Excellent Palace and Dominions, Home of Vishnu and All the Gods'.

It is a tongue-twister, even for Thais, who shorten it to 'Krungthep' or the 'City of Angels' in everyday speech. The international community, following the preference of foreign ambassadors to the Chakri court, uses 'Bangkok'.

With a population of around 10 million, Bangkok is about 40 times larger than Nakhon Ratchasima or Chiang Mai, Thailand's next largest towns. It has a reputation for traffic jams, although the situation is improving yearly. It is also a city of culture, haute cuisine and a throbbing, thrilling nightlife while being surprisingly safe and welcoming.

One of the stranger features of Bangkok is the absence of any single centre. The old royal city, built within three concentric canals on Ratanakosin Island, is the cultural and historical heart. Downtown Silom Road and the surrounding area are the equivalent of Bangkok's Wall Street – here are the major banking and trading institutions, as well as, near Silom's eastern end, the world-famous entertainment area Patpong Road, now known as much for its night market as for its neon lights and go-go bars. Sukhumvit Road, stretching away east towards Pattaya and the Gulf Coast, is a shopper's paradise, as well as a preferred location for many expatriate residents and mid-budget visitors.

A porter at Pak Khlong Talad, Bangkok

Bangkok has become a city of gleaming shopping malls, best exemplified by the Mahboonkrong Centre, World Trade Centre and the region around Siam Square. Yet it is also still a city of canals, dominated by the great Chao Phraya River, which neatly bisects the Thai capital on its way to the nearby Gulf of Siam.

What to See in Bangkok

BANGKOK'S CANALS AND RIVER ✪✪

Bangkok was built on a bend in the Maenam Chao Phraya or 'River of Kings'. It had few roads, but was criss-crossed by canals, called *khlong* in Thai. In Thonburi, to the west of the river, a network of canals has survived. These were – and are – active canals, now used for commerce, commuting and tourist rides on long-tail speedboats. Easily chartered at any of the numerous piers, the long-tail boats dart up narrow canals, enabling passengers to explore little-known riverside communities. Alternatively, visitors can dine in state aboard a converted rice barge as it sails past majestic Wat Arun and the Grand Palace (► 18). The regular ferry service that runs throughout the city all day is the cheapest way to explore the Chao Phraya.

CHATUCHAK WEEKEND MARKET (► 16, TOP TEN)

CHINATOWN ✪

Yaowarat, or Chinatown, is a seething warren of busy market streets, Chinese shrines, gold shops and great Chinese restaurants. A stroll along narrow Sampeng Lane, the heart of old Chinatown, is recommended.

Sunset Cruise
✚ 34B1
✉ Marriott Royal Garden Riverside Hotel, Thanon Charoen Nakhon
☎ (02) 476 0021
🕐 Daily 5:30PM
💷 Moderate

Riverside Company (dinner cruises)
✚ Off map
✉ From Krungthon Bridge, Thanon Ratchawithi
☎ (02) 434 0090
🕐 Daily 7:30PM
💷 Moderate

✚ 34B2
✉ Sampeng Lane area
🕐 Daily
🍴 Yau Wah Yuen (££)
🚌 1, 7

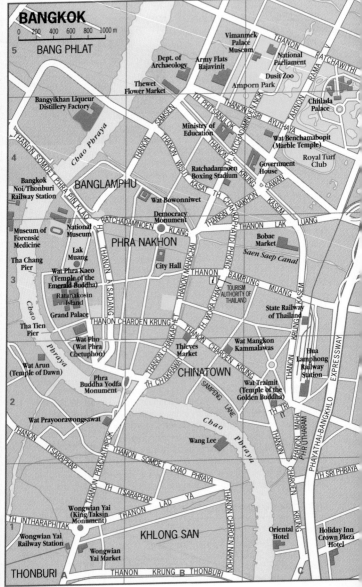

BANGKOK

0   200   400   600   800   1000 m

BANG PHLAT

Vimanmek Palace Museum

National Parliament

Dept. of Archaeology

Army Flats Rajavinit

Dusit Zoo

Amporn Park

Thewet Flower Market

Chitlada Palace

Bangyikhan Liqueur Distillery Factory

Chao Phraya

THANON SOMDET PHRA PIN KLAO

Ministry of Education

Wat Benchamabopit (Marble Temple)

Royal Turf Club

Ratchadamnoen Boxing Stadium

Government House

Bangkok Noi/Thonburi Railway Station

BANGLAMPHU

Wat Bowonniwet

Democracy Monument

RATCHADAMNOEN KLANG

Museum of Forensic Medicine

National Museum

PHRA NAKHON

Bobae Market

Saen Saep Canal

Lak Muang

Tha Chang Pier

Wat Phra Kaeo (Temple of the Emerald Buddha)

City Hall

THANON

BAMRUNG MUANG

TOURISM AUTHORITY OF THAILAND

Ratanakosin Island

Grand Palace

State Railway of Thailand

THANON CHAROEN KRUNG

Tha Tien Pier

Chao Phraya

Wat Pho (Wat Phra Chetuphon)

Wat Mangkon Kammalawas

Hua Lamphong Railway Station

Wat Arun (Temple of Dawn)

Thieves Market

CHINATOWN

Phra Buddha Yodfa Monument

SAMPENG LANE

Wat Traimit (Temple of the Golden Buddha)

EXPRESSWAY

Wat Prayoorawongsawat

Chao Phraya

THANON ITSARAPHAP

Wang Lee

THANON PRACHATHIPOK

THANON SOMDET CHAO PHRAYA

THANON ITSARAPHAP

LAD YA

Wongwian Yai (King Taksin Monument)

Oriental Hotel

Holiday Inn Crown Plaza Hotel

Wongwian Yai Railway Station

KHLONG SAN

Wongwian Yai Market

THONBURI

THANON KRUNG THONBURI

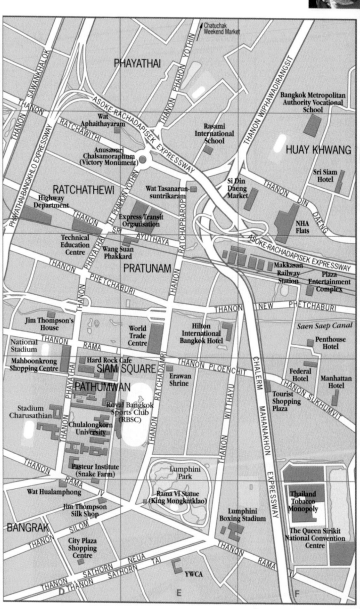

35E2
Thanon Ploenchit
Daily
Cafés, Sogo Department Store
4, 5
E1 Chidlom Station
None
Free

Below: *inside Jim Thompson's House*

35D3
Soi Kasemsan 2, off Thanon Rama I
(02) 216 7368
Mon–Sat 9–5
National Stadium
8
Few
Moderate

ERAWAN SHRINE ✪

Many shrines are scattered throughout Bangkok but the most famous is dedicated to the four-headed Hindu deity Brahma *(Phra Prohm* in Thai). Constructed to dispel bad luck during the building of the Erawan Hotel in the 1950s, the shrine proved an immense success and believers still flock to pay their respects from all over the city. The atmosphere is rich with the fragrance of jasmine and incense, and elegant shrine dancers perform to a traditional Thai orchestra whenever someone pays them to do so. Entry is free but most visitors offer some flowers and incense; many believe that those who do so will be blessed with good luck and return to the 'City of Angels'.

GRAND PALACE (▶ 18–19, TOP TEN)

JIM THOMPSON'S HOUSE ✪✪✪

American businessman Jim Thompson set up in Thailand shortly after World War II and, almost single-handedly, revived the traditional Thai silk industry. This avid collector of antiquities, not just from Thailand but from Myanmar (Burma), Laos and Cambodia, built a magnificent house (actually several traditional central Thai wooden houses) at the end of a quiet lane by the banks of the Saen Saep Canal. Thompson disappeared mysteriously in Malaysia in 1967 but his elegant house has become a trust property.

NATIONAL MUSEUM ⊗⊗

This is one of the largest and best-stocked museums in Southeast Asia, with a remarkable collection of objects from all periods of known 'Thai' history – that is, from Ban Chiang civilisation more than 4,000 years ago, through the Mon and Khmer periods, to the eventual immigration and settlement of the various Thai-speaking peoples from about AD 900 onwards. As might be expected, the displays on the golden eras of Thai history – the Sukhothai and Ayuthaya periods – are particularly strong. The museum is well maintained and well presented, and regular guided tours are available.

✚ 34A4
✉ Thanon Na Phra That
☎ (02) 224 1370
🕐 Wed–Sun 9–4
🍴 Wang Ngar Restaurant
🚌 7, 9, 11, 39
♿ Few
💰 Cheap

Above: *the National Museum*

ORIENTAL HOTEL ⊗

Beautifully situated by the banks of the Chao Phraya River, the Oriental consistently rates in international surveys among the top five hotels in the world. Although expensive to stay in, the Oriental offers excellent restaurants with riverside views and, most interestingly, the 'Writers' Room', once frequented by luminaries such as Joseph Conrad, Somerset Maugham, Noel Coward and Graham Greene.

✚ 34C1
✉ 48 Soi Oriental
☎ (02) 659 9000
🚇 S6 Saphan Taksin Station
🚌 2, 4, 5
♿ Very Good

Ko Ratanakosin

Distance
2.5km

Time
2–4 hours, depending on temple visits

Start point
Lak Muang, Thanon Ratchadamnoen Nai
✚ 34A3
🚌 7, 9, 11

End point
The Grand Palace
✚ 34A3

Lunch
Lan Theh (£)
✉ Tha Maharat Pier, Chao Phraya River

The carved form and benevolent face of a whiskered statue, among the many sights at Wat Arun

This walk encompasses the central part of historic Bangkok, known to the Thais as Ko Ratanakosin (Ratanakosin Island) because it is isolated from the rest of the city by a network of canals connecting with the Chao Phraya River.

Begin your walk at the Lak Muang or city pillar, traditionally regarded as the heart of the city. Situated at the intersection of Thanon Ratchadamnoen Nai and Thanon Lak Muang, this shrine is best reached by taxi.

From Lak Muang walk south with the Grand Palace walls to your right. Turn right along Thanon Chetuphon and after about 500m you will reach the impressive entrance to Wat Pho.

Officially known as Wat Phra Chetuphon, this is Bangkok's oldest and grandest temple, with a spectacular reclining Buddha. It is also renowned for its massage school, and visitors can enjoy a relaxing and invigorating traditional massage at a very reasonable price.

After leaving Wat Pho head north along Thanon Maharat beside the river to Tha Tien pier. Here catch a cross-river ferry to Wat Arun, which dominates the far bank.

Wat Arun or the 'Temple of Dawn' has a striking, Khmer-style *prang* or spire, virtually the whole of which is decorated with shards of porcelain. Be warned, though, the steps are steep and narrow – if you suffer from vertigo, avoid the climb.

From Wat Arun cross back to Ratanakosin Island and continue north along Maharat Road. Near Tha Chang pier turn right onto Thanon Na Phra Lan. Enter the Grand Palace's main entrance.

The Grand Palace and its adjacent temple, Wat Phra Kaeo, are outstanding examples of early Ratanakosin architecture. You are relatively free to wander about, but dress respectfully and do not photograph the Emerald Buddha.

Below: *one of five raised traditional Thai houses in the grounds of Wang Suan Phakkard*

VIMANMEK PALACE ✪✪

Originally constructed for King Chulalongkorn in 1868, Vimanmek was moved to its present location near Dusit Palace in 1910. A three-storey mansion comprising more than 80 rooms, Vimanmek is reputedly the largest golden teak building in the world. Certainly the cost of assembling a similar structure today would be astronomical. The interior contains an extensive collection of early Ratanakosin dynasty objects and numerous antiques from the late 19th century.

✚ 34C5
✉ Thanon U-Thong Nai
☎ (02) 281 4715
🕐 Daily 9:30–3
🚻 10
♿ Few
💰 Cheap

WANG SUAN PHAKKARD ✪✪

The 'Lettuce Farm Palace', as this charming building is known in Thai, was the residence of Princess Chumbot of Nakhon Sawan in the 1950s. An important scion of the ruling Thai royal family, Princess Chumbot was an eminent art collector and patron of Thai culture. Like Jim Thompson's House, the complex contains magnificent artistic treasures, including a fine lacquered pavilion dating from the late Ayuthaya period. Its beautifully landscaped gardens are a tranquil oasis in downtown Bangkok.

✚ 35E3
✉ 352 Thanon Sri Ayuthaya
🕐 Mon–Sat 9–4
🚇 N2 Phya Thai Station
🚌 2, 3, 4
♿ Good
💰 Moderate

BUR Burma (Myanmar)

CENTRAL
THAILAND

K Cambodia

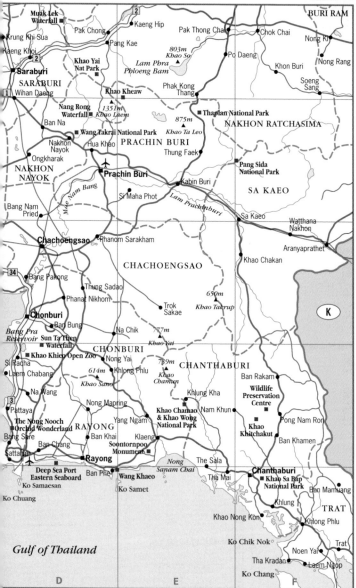

BURI RAM

Muak Lek Waterfall
Pak Chong
Kaeng Hip
Pak Thong Chai
Chok Chai
Nong Ki
Krung Khi Sua
Pang Kae
803m
Khao So
Po Daeng
Nong Rang
Kaeng Khoi
Khon Buri
Khao Yai Nat Park
Lam Phra Phloeng Bam
Phak Kong Thang
Soeng Sang
Saraburi
SARABURI
Wihan Daeng
Khao Kheaw
Nang Rong Waterfall
1351m
Khao Laem
Thaplan National Park
NAKHON RATCHASIMA
Ban Na
875m
Wang Takrai National Park
Khao Ta Leo
Nakhon Nayok
Hua Khao
PRACHIN BURI
Thung Faek
Ongkharak
NAKHON NAYOK
Prachin Buri
Pang Sida National Park
Kabin Buri
SA KAEO
Mae Nam Bang
Si Maha Phot
Lam Prachinburi
Bang Nam Pried
Sa Kaeo
Watthana Nakhon
Chachoengsao
Phanom Sarakham
Aranyaprathet
CHACHOENGSAO
Khao Chakan
Bang Pakong
650m
Khao Takrup
Thung Sadao
Phanat Nikhom
Trok Sakae
K
Chonburi
Ban Bung
Na Chik
777m
Khao Yai
Bang Pra Reservoir
Sun Ta Then Waterfall
CHONBURI
739m
Khao Khieo Open Zoo
Nong Yai
Khao Channan
CHANTHABURI
Ban Rakam
Si Radha
614m
Khlong Phlu
Khlung Kha
Wildlife Preservation Centre
Laem Chabang
Khao Sano
Nam Khun
Pong Nam Ron
Na Wang
Nong Mapring
Khao Chanao & Khao Wong National Park
Khao Khitchakut
Pattaya
Yang Ngam
RAYONG
Ban Khamen
The Nong Nooch Orchid Wonderland
Ban Khai
Klaeng
Bang Sare
Ban Chang
Soontornpoo Monument
Nong Sanam Chai
The Sala
Chanthaburi
Sattahip
Rayong
Tha Mai
Khao Sa Bap National Park
Deep Sea Port Eastern Seaboard
Ban Phe
Wang Khaeo
Ban Mamuang
Ko Samaesan
Khlung
TRAT
Ko Chuang
Ko Samet
Khao Nong Kon
Khlong Phlu
Ko Chik Nok
Noen Yai
Trat
Gulf of Thailand
Tha Kradan
Laem Ngop
Ko Chang

D   E   F

What to See in Central Thailand

AYUTHAYA ●●●

- 40C4
- 86km north of Bangkok
- Regular air-conditioned buses from Bangkok

In 1351 King Ramathibodi established his new capital at a former Khmer outpost on an island in the Chao Phraya River, symbolising both the permanent transfer of Siamese power from Sukhothai to the south and the decline of the Cambodian Empire. He called his new city Ayuthaya – in Sanskrit 'unassailable' – after the town of Ayodhya in India. For the next 416 years Ayuthaya was the capital of Siam, finally proving all too assailable when it was captured by Burmese armies in 1767.

Bang Pa In

- 40C4
- 20km south of Ayuthaya
- Daily 9–3
- Few
- Moderate

The new Siamese leader, King Taksin, moved his capital to Thonburi, from where it was transferred to Bangkok after Taksin's execution in 1782. Many of the new buildings in Bangkok employed materials floated downstream by raft from the ruins of Ayuthaya but the once-splendid city still retains an aura of royalty and some remarkable historical monuments. It is easy to visit from Bangkok – a popular way to do so is by luxurious riverboat, dining en route and stopping to visit King Chulalongkorn's palace at Bang Pa In.

Chan Kasem Palace National Museum

- 43C3
- Thanon U Thong, Ayuthaya
- Wed–Sun 9–12, 1–4
- Chainam (£)
- Songthaew, tuk-tuk
- Few
- Cheap

An excellent way to gain an impression of the size and grandeur of Ayuthaya's majestic ruins is to rent a local long-tail boat and make a complete circuit of the island.

In the northeastern part of Ayuthaya, the Chan Kasem

Chao Sam Phraya National Museum

- 42B1
- Thanon Rotchana, Ayuthaya
- Wed–Sun 9–4
- Songthaew, tuk-tuk
- Few
- Cheap

Wat Mongkhon Bophit

- 42B2
- Thanon Si Sanphet, Ayuthaya
- Daily 8–6:30
- Songthaew, tuk-tuk
- Few
- Moderate

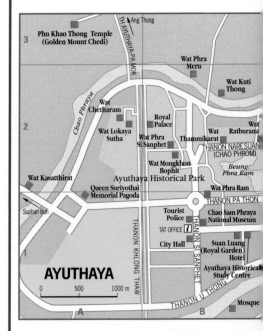

Palace National Museum displays Buddhist art and treasures. Built by King Maha Thammarat (1569–90) for his son, the palace was destroyed by the Burmese in 1767 but restored by King Mongkut in the mid-19th century.

Ayuthaya's largest museum, the Chao Sam Phraya National Museum, is in the middle of town. The collection includes many of the best pieces to have survived the Burmese sack of Ayuthaya, especially Thai Buddhist sculpture and religious imagery. Books on Thai religious art and Ayuthaya history are for sale here.

A long line of Buddhas at the restored Wat Yai Chai Mongkhon

Ayuthaya is packed with old temples, but Wat Mongkhon Bophit is rather special because of its huge, numinous black Buddha image. Cast in the 15th century, this unique work of art was for many years exposed to the elements, but since 1956 has been protected by a brick and stucco building. The effect of entering the building and looking up into the gilded eyes of the huge black Buddha figure can leave quite an impression.

AYUTHAYA HISTORICAL PARK ✪✪✪

This UNESCO World Heritage Site covers most of the island and has many temples worth visiting, so a minimum of half a day is required (a full day, with lunch by the river would be ideal). Bicycles can be rented near the park entrance.

🔢 40C4
✉ 86km north of Bangkok
🕐 Daily 9–4
🚌 *Songthaew, tuk-tuk* from Thanon Si Sanphet
☎ (035) 245123–4
♿ Few
💵 Moderate
❓ Among the many temples worth visiting are Wat Mongkhon Bophit, Wat Phra Si Sanphet, Wat Phra Mahathat, Wat Ratburana and Wat Yai Chai Mongkhon

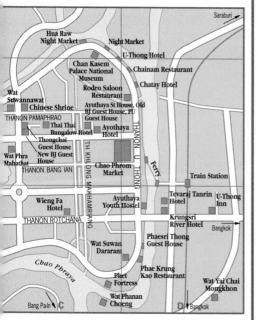

40C3/4

Bang Khu Wiang,
Thonburi

Daily 4AM–7:30AM

Long-tail boat from pier
near Wat Phra Kaeo

Few

Free

BANG KHU WIANG FLOATING MARKET ⭐⭐

Few experiences are more authentically Thai than a visit to
a floating market. The best known is at Bang Khu Wiang in
Thonburi, on the west bank of the Chao Phraya River.
Water-borne commerce, most of which is conducted by
women, starts at the crack of dawn and goes on for
usually no more than two or three hours. To see Bang Khu
Wiang, charter a long-tail boat from Tha Chang on
Bangkok's Ratanakosin Island at about 6AM.

A better, busier and more authentic floating market
near Bangkok is at Damnoen Saduak (➤ 46).

There was a time, especially in the flat and well-
watered central plains, when most commerce was
water-borne. This is no longer true – canals have been
filled in and built over, roads and covered markets have
been constructed and scarcely a town in Thailand is
without supermarkets and shopping malls. Floating
markets – *talaat naam* in Thai – are now perceived to be a
useful and lucrative tourist attraction.

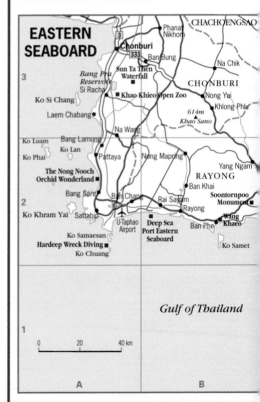

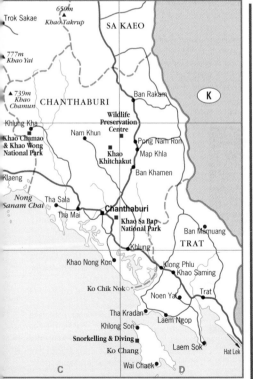

*Early morning at
Damnoen Saduak
floating market*

K Cambodia

Map labels:
Trok Sakae
650m
Khao Takrup
SA KAEO
777m
Khao Yai
▲739m
*Khao
Chamun*
CHANTHABURI
Ban Rakam
K
Khlung Kha
Wildlife
Preservation
Centre
Nam Khun
**Khao Chamao
& Khao Wong
National Park**
Pong Nam Ron
■ **Khao
Khitchakut**
Map Khla
Ban Khamen
Klaeng
*Nong
Sanam Chai*
Tha Sala
Tha Mai
Chanthaburi
**Khao Sa Bap
National Park**
Ban Mamuang
Khlung
TRAT
Khao Nong Kon
Klong Phlu
Khao Saming
Ko Chik Nok
Noen Ya
Trat
Tha Kradan
Laem Ngop
Khlong Son
Snorkelling & Diving ■
Laem Sok
Ko Chang
Hat Lek
Wai Chaek
C
D

+ 45C2
⊠ 330km southeast of Bangkok
🚌 Regular air-conditioned buses from Bangkok
♿ None
↔ Khao Khitchakut National Park
  ⊠ 28km northeast of Chanthaburi
  ☎ (039) 431983

+ 40B3
⊠ Damnoen Saduak, 104km southwest of Bangkok
🕐 Daily from sunrise
🍴 Snacks sold from boats
🚌 78 from southern bus terminal, Bangkok
🚤 Water taxi from Damnoen Saduak to Talaat Phitak
♿ None

+ 44/45
⊠ East of Bangkok
🚌 Regular air-conditioned buses from Bangkok to all towns

Holidaymakers relax under thatched shelters on the beach at Pattaya

CHANTHABURI ✪

This busy riverside commercial hub specialising in the gem trade (both local and imported from the Pailin region in Cambodia) is home to 40,000 people. It is famous for its fine fruits, especially durian, rambutan, langsat, pineapple and mangosteen. Chanthaburi ('City of the Moon') has historical links with France and Vietnam and features shophouse architecture influenced by these nations. Many residents are of Vietnamese descent and are Catholic (the city has Thailand's largest cathedral.).

DAMNOEN SADUAK FLOATING MARKET ✪

Take a water taxi to the floating market on Khlong Damnoen Saduak in Ratchaburi Province, 104km southwest of Bangkok (after first going to Damnoen Saduak by bus or taxi). As with all morning markets in Thailand, it is best to arrive as early as possible (certainly by 8:30AM). Even at dawn, the market is busy, as boats laden with an extensive range of fruit, vegetables and flowers jostle for space on the crowded waterway.

THE EASTERN GULF COAST ✪✪✪

Thailand's eastern gulf coast is something of a contradiction. On the one hand, it is the nation's most developed commercial region, with Laem Chabang deep-water port, oil refineries and an ugly industrial zone stretching east and south from Bangkok for almost 100km. On the other hand, it has some of the finest beaches in Thailand, the delightful island of Ko Samet and, in and around Ko Chang ('Elephant Island'), one of the least-developed, most pristine archipelagos in Southeast Asia.

One of the area's attractions is its proximity to Bangkok, but this has a downside. Good roads make it readily accessible – there is an elevated freeway stretching as far as Chonburi. Resorts nearer to Bangkok are generally packed, particularly on weekends. There is not a lot to interest visitors in Chachoengsao and Chonburi, and most people prefer to head south to the coastal resorts. The first of these, Si Racha, is largely a Thai destination, while the next, Pattaya, is geared towards foreign visitors. Next comes Rayong, jumping-off point for Ko Samet and increasingly a resort town in its own right.

Further east is the fascinating old town of Chanthaburi. The road east, Sukhumvit Highway, ends in a tapering finger of Thailand that culminates in the quintessentially Thai city of Trat (certainly not a resort town), the Ko Chang archipelago and the small town of Hat Lek, an official crossing point into Cambodia.

Buddhist monks bathing at Erawan National Park

ERAWAN NATIONAL PARK ●●

This park covers 550sq km of unspoilt wilderness in the Khwae Yai river valley. It is a great place for walking and swimming, with well-marked trails and numerous water-falls, the highest of which is named after the mythical Hindu-Buddhist three-headed elephant Erawan.

The best time to visit is during the rainy season when the falls are at their most impressive, but, being quite close to Bangkok, the park is a popular draw for local visitors and is best avoided during *songkran*, the traditional Thai New Year each April, if you are seeking solitude and empty spaces.

40A4

✉ 65km northwest of Kanchanaburi

☎ (02) 579 7223

♿ Few

🎟 Cheap

JEATH WAR MUSEUM ●

The acronym by which this interesting war museum is known represents the first letters of the combatant nations – Japan, England, Australia, America, Thailand and Holland. A friendly Thai monk called Phra Tongproh, who speaks some English, runs the museum and he can be very helpful in showing visitors around. The museum is based on one of the *atap* huts in which Allied prisoners of war were held during World War II. Exhibits on display include paintings by former prisoners, photographs and various weapons, such as Japanese swords.

40A4

✉ Thanon Wissutharangsi, Kanchanaburi

🕐 Daily 8:30–6

♿ Few

🎟 Cheap

DID YOU KNOW?

A long-tail boat is a fast boat with a long propeller shaft projecting about 2m from the stern. The propeller shaft swings freely and is used for steering.

40A4
130km west of Bangkok
Mae Nam (££)
Regular air-conditioned buses from Bangkok
Kanchanaburi Station

Death Railway Bridge
Thanon Mae Nam Kwai, Kanchanaburi
Unrestricted
Songthaew
None
Free
River Kwai Bridge Week, late Nov

Allied War Cemeteries
Thanon Saengchuto, Kanchanaburi
Unrestricted
Minibus No.2
Good
Free

KANCHANABURI ✪✪

The small town of Kanchanaburi is a delightful place, ironically with a worldwide reputation for the notorious 'bridge over the river Kwai'. During World War II, the invading Japanese forces decided to build a supply railway link across the difficult country between the Thai and Burmese rail systems. Hundreds of thousands of people were forced to work under appalling conditions, resulting in the deaths of an estimated 16,000 Allied prisoners of war and 100,000 indentured Asians.

The original bridge was destroyed by Allied bombing during 1945 and only rebuilt after the war. Today little remains of the original railway to Myanmar (Burma), although trains can still run within Thailand as far as Nam Tok via the infamous 'Hellfire Pass'.

Most visitors to Kanchanaburi go to see the bridge and perhaps to pay their respects at the war cemeteries – the Kanchanaburi Allied War Cemetery in the north-central part of town, and the more distant Chung Kai Allied War Cemetery on the west bank of the Kwai River. Reaching this cemetery involves a short boat trip and a pleasant stroll through unspoilt rural Thailand. Both cemeteries are well cared for and contain the graves of thousands of Dutch, British, French, New Zealand and Australian soldiers.

Top and right: *the bridge across the River Kwai*
Above: *the Allied War Cemeteries*

Majestic mountains watch over the waterside buildings of Kanchanaburi at dawn

'Kan' has good accommodation and a wide choice of restaurants. Like most Thai cities, it has a city pillar (the Lak Meuang) at its symbolic heart. Found near the post office, the pillar has a bulbous-shaped tip, sometimes likened to a lotus but generally accepted as phallic in origin, which devotees have covered in gold leaf.

One of the more unusual sights in Kanchanaburi, indeed in Thailand, is at Wat Tham Mongkon Thong, the 'Temple of the Cave of the Golden Dragon'. The temple itself is nothing special but is famed throughout Thailand for its 'floating nun'. This entails the unusual spectacle of a Thai *mae chii* or nun floating on her back while meditating in a pool of water. Pious Buddhists come to witness this act and to receive the nun's blessings.

Kanchanaburi is a rewarding destination at any time of the year, but the best time is in late November and early December when a series of *son-et-lumières* based around the restored bridge is held daily.

The floating nun
- ✉ Thanon Chukkadon, across Mae Klong River, Kanchanaburi
- 🕐 Daily 7–6
- ♿ Few
- 🎫 Free (donation)

✚ 45D1
✉ 350km southeast of Bangkok
🍴 Excellent beach cafés
🚌 Air-conditioned buses from Bangkok
♿ None

KO CHANG ✪✪

Ko Chang (Elephant Island) is the biggest of more than 40 islands in the Gulf of Siam, off the coast of Trat, Thailand's most southeasterly province. It is Thailand's second largest island after Phuket but almost completely undeveloped by comparison. Until recently it had no paved roads, and accommodation is still limited to simple bungalows scattered along the coast. Best reached by ferry from Laem Ngop, it is a wonderland of unspoilt tropical rainforest, pristine beaches and clear seas – but light on the water sports available at more developed resorts.

✚ 44B2
✉ 220km southeast of Bangkok, Gulf of Thailand
🍴 Excellent beach cafés
🚌 Regular buses from Bangkok to Ban Phe
♿ None
 Cheap
 Laem Ya–Ko Samet National Park

KO SAMET ✪✪

This narrow finger of an island lying just a short distance off the coast of Rayong is still, despite its increasing popularity, a relaxing destination. Distinguished by remarkably white, crisp beaches, it offers sunbathing, swimming, snorkelling and excellent seafood. For nightlife, go to Pattaya instead.

Visitors strolling along a pristine beach at Ko Samet

✚ 44A2
✉ 147km southeast of Bangkok
🍴 Good restaurants
🚌 Bangkok Airport minibuses, regular air-conditioned buses
♿ Few
 Pattaya Station
❓ Pattaya Festival, 12–19 Apr

PATTAYA ✪

Visitors usually develop very definite opinions about this place. Long billed as Thailand's top resort, the beaches are poor compared with Phuket, Ko Samui and Ko Samet. On the other hand, the sheer number of hotels, restaurants and entertainment venues is staggering. Long infamous for its nightlife, the southern part of town is packed with bars and bar girls – there is a big homosexual scene, too. Northern Pattaya, however, is much more of a family destination, as is Jomtien Beach, stretching to the south of the city.

Lopburi

The busy town of Lopburi, about 150km north of Bangkok, has a long history. Originally settled by Mon people, it was an important bastion of Dvaravati culture from as early as AD 600, before being conquered, in turn, by the Khmer Empire and the Thais. In the mid-17th century Lopburi was used as a second capital by King Narai, who built a summer palace there.

Today Lopburi is conveniently divided into western and eastern sections. The former includes the old town as well as earlier Khmer ruins. To the east the new town is the site of the provincial offices and the best hotels.

Start a walk around Lopburi at Narai's palace, which was abandoned soon after his death and not restored until the mid-19th century. The palace exhibits both French and Khmer architectural influences, as well as Central Thai.

Enter Narai's palace through the main gate (Pratu Phayakkha) and stroll through the well-kept grounds. To the left are the elephant stables.

The palace took 12 years to build (1665–77), and comprised a royal temple, harem buildings, audience halls, administrative buildings and kitchens. The Lopburi National Museum here has an outstanding collection of Mon and Khmer period statuary. To the east of the palace grounds is Wat Phra Si Ratana Mahathat, a 12th-century Khmer temple restored by the Fine Arts Department.

Walk east a short distance to the railroad station, then north along Thanon Na Phra Kan.

To the right is Wat Nakhon Kosa, a 12th-century Khmer temple, which may once have been dedicated to Hinduism.

Keep walking north across the roundabout.

In the middle of the roundabout is San Phra Kan, a shrine dedicated to Kala, the Hindu god of death and time. The shrine swarms with the monkeys for which Lopburi is famous. They can be bad-tempered so avoid being bitten!

Continue north along Thanon Na Phra Kan.

On the right is Prang Sam Yot, another Khmer-built Hindu temple that has long since been dedicated to Buddhism.

Sidebar

✚ 40C5

Distance
12.5km

Time
1–2 hours

Start point
Narai's Palace
🚏 Songthaew

End point
Prang Sam Yot

Lunch
Boon Bakery (£)
✉ Thanon Na Phra Kan

Monkeys in the grounds of Wat Phra Prang Sam Yot

In the Know

If your time in Thailand is limited, or you would like to get a real flavour of the country, here are some ideas:

10 Ways to be a Thai

Have fun – the general attitude of Thais is that if something is not *sanuk* (fun) it is not worth doing.

Stay cool, as overt displays of public affection or, far worse, anger, are frowned upon; smile and keep your temper at all times.

Show respect for the monarchy, especially King Bhumibol and his grandfather, King Chulalongkorn (Rama V).

Show respect for religion, especially Buddhism and Buddha images. Do not climb on the latter to take photos.

Try a traditional Thai massage – the contortions and manipulations involved are designed to reduce tension.

Drink some Thai whisky, such as the popular brand, Mekong, taken with soda, ice and fresh lemon or sometimes Coca-Cola.

Watch *sepak takraw*, a kind of volleyball with a rattan ball played with the feet and head. It is popular among Thais.

Dress appropriately, especially in temples. Nudity and topless sunbathing on the beach are considered offensive.

Learn some Thai – even a few words will win smiles.

Try Thai food, which is delicious, sophisticated and sometimes spicy.

10 Good Places to Have Lunch

Border View (££) ✉ 222 Golden Triangle, Sop Ruak ☎ (053) 784001–5. Thai, Chinese and Western food presented on a beautiful terrace by the Mekong.

The limestone cliffs of Rai Leh at Krabi, one of the best rock-climbing sites in Southeast Asia

Bussaracum (£££) ✉ 139 Sethiwan Building, Thanon Pun, Bangkok ☎ (02) 266 6312. Enjoy royal Thai cuisine in an elegant atmosphere.

Captain's Choice (£££) ✉ Choeng Mon Beach, Ko Samui ☎ (07) 425041. One of Samui's top restaurants, renowned for its fresh seafood.

Giorgio's (££) ✉ Beach Road, Patong Beach, Pattaya ☎ (076) 341193. Italian food and good

One of the quietest is Mai Khao.
Swimming in Thailand's warm, clear seas, especially in the south.
Walking on signposted trails in national parks.

Top Adventure Activities

Big-game fishing off Phuket, Krabi and Trang.
Boating/sea canoeing – explore the sea caves and karst towers at Phang-nga.
Caving around Chiang Mai and Mae Hong Son.
Diving or snorkelling in the pristine Andaman Sea.
Elephant riding through the lush Mae Sa Valley.
Mountain biking in and around Chiang Mai.
Parasailing is always popular, especially at Pattaya and Phuket.
Rock climbing at Phang-nga Bay and the peninsular south.
Trekking to see the north's hill tribes, especially from November to February.
White-water rafting is popular in Chiang Rai and the north.

wines served in a beautiful tropical garden.
Indochine (££) ✉ Wat Jaeng, Thanon Samphasit, Ubon Ratchathani ☎ (045) 245584. One of Thailand's best Vietnamese restaurants, in an old teak house.
Le Coq d'Or (£££) ✉ 68/1 Thanon Ko Klang, Chiang Mai ☎ (053) 282024. This top French restaurant was formerly the British consul's residence.
Lemongrass (££) ✉ 5/1 Soi 24 Thanon Sukhumvit, Bangkok ☎ (02) 258 8637. Fine Thai food served in an elegant, old, wooden house.
Lobster Pot (£££) ✉ 288 Beach Road, Pattaya ☎ (038) 426083. Fine seafood in the heart of downtown Pattaya.
Riverside (££) ✉ 9/11 Thanon Charoen Rat, Chiang Mai ☎ (053) 243239. Good Thai and European food; excellent live music.
Tum Nak Thai (££) ✉ 131 Thanon Ratchadapisek, Bangkok ☎ (02) 274 6420. Perhaps the largest restaurant in the

Khukhut Waterbird Sanctuary, 30km north of Songkhla

world – the staff use rollerskates. Good for kids.

Top Activities

Bird-watching by the Mekong, in the mountainous north and by the south's lagoons.
Dancing at world-class discos in Bangkok, Phuket, Ko Samui and Chiang Mai.
Golfing on the country's many fine courses.
Thai cooking lessons – there are plenty of schools, especially in Chiang Mai.
Learn Thai massage and apply the skills back home!
Go river fishing – try your luck with a Mekong catfish.
Shopping – particularly in Bangkok and Chiang Mai.
Sunbathing on some of the world's best beaches, including Kata, Phra Nang, Chaweng and Maya Bay.

Golf is a popular pastime all over Thailand

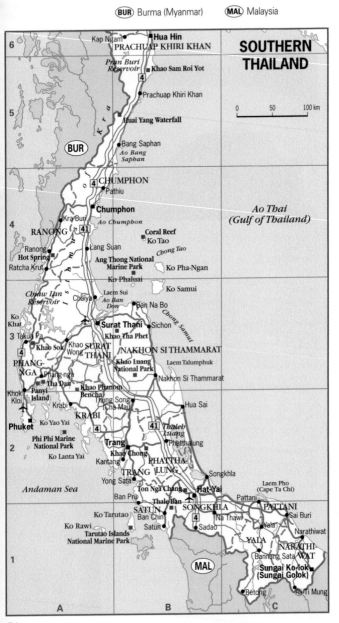

BUR Burma (Myanmar)   **MAL** Malaysia

SOUTHERN THAILAND

0   50   100 km

6 — Kap Ngam · **Hua Hin** ■
PRACHUAP KHIRI KHAN
Pran Buri Reservoir · ■ Khao Sam Roi Yot
[4]
· Prachuap Khiri Khan

5 — **Huai Yang Waterfall**

BUR · Bang Saphan
Ao Bang Saphan

[4] ● CHUMPHON
· Pathiu

· Chumphon
Ao Chumphon *Ao Thai (Gulf of Thailand)*

4 — Kra Buri
RANONG [41]
· Ranong   · Lang Suan   Coral Reef
Hot Spring   ● Ko Tao
Ratcha Krut ·   *Chong Tao*
Ang Thong National
Marine Park   ● Ko Pha-Ngan
· Ko Phaluai
Chiaw Larn Reservoir Chaiya   Laem Sui   Ko Samui
Ao Ban Don   · Ban Na Bo
Ko   · Sichon   *Chong Samui*
Khat   · Takua Pa   ● **Surat Thani**
Khao Tha Phet
3 — Khao Sok   SURAT   NAKHON SI THAMMARAT
Khao   THANI
Wong   Khao Luang   Laem Talumphuk
PHANG-   National Park
NGA   · Nakhon Si Thammarat
Phang-nga
· Tha Dan   Khao Phanom
Khok   Panyi   Bencha
Kloi   Island   Thung Song   · Hua Sai
· Krabi   (Cha-Mai)
Phuket ● Ko Yao Yai   KRABI
[4]   [41] *Thaleh Luang*
Phi Phi Marine   ● **Trang**   · Phatthalung
2 — National Park   Khao Chong   PHATTHA-
Ko Lanta Yai   Kantang   LUNG
TRANG · LUNG
Andaman Sea   Yong Sata   Ton Nga Chang   ● **Hat-Yai**
Ban Pru   · Songkhla
Laem Pho
(Cape Ta Chi)
SATUN   Thale Ban   SONGKHLA   · Pattani
Ko Tarutao   Ban Chin   [4]   PATTANI
· Satun   · Na Thawi   · Sai Buri
Ko Rawi   Sadao   YALA · Yala
1 — Tarutao Islands   · Narathiwat
National Marine Park   NARATHI-
WAT
Bannang Sata ■
MAL   **Sungai Ko-lok**
(Sungai Golok) ■
· Betong   · Ali Ti Mung

A   B   C

Southern Thailand

Southern, peninsular Thailand is a narrow strip of land, likened to an elephant's trunk, which joins the bulk of mainland Southeast Asia to the Malay Peninsula via the Isthmus of Kra. It is a beautiful region of coconut palms and rubber plantations, azure lagoons and sharp karst outcrops. Some Thais believe southerners are more fiery in disposition than their fellow citizens. There is little to indicate this to the visitor except perhaps the spicier food and the speed at which the local dialect of Thai is spoken.

In this part of Thailand, Buddhist culture persists as far south as Nakhon Si Thammarat, then Islam begins to appear. By the time you reach Phuket, the blend of traditions is obvious. Chinese settlers, too, have left a major mark on this region. Finally, in the four 'deep south' provinces of Pattani, Yala, Narathiwat and Satun, Islam becomes predominant and Malay is the main local language. Here Thai and Malay worlds meet and merge in an unusual and successful synthesis of cultures.

> *'On the edge of the canals, especially near the coast, luscious tropical vegetation reigns. The overhanging bamboo clumps and high-rise palms offer beautiful landscapes enlivened by the occasional houses...'*

KARL DOHRING, *(on Southern Thailand)*
The Country and People of Siam (1923)

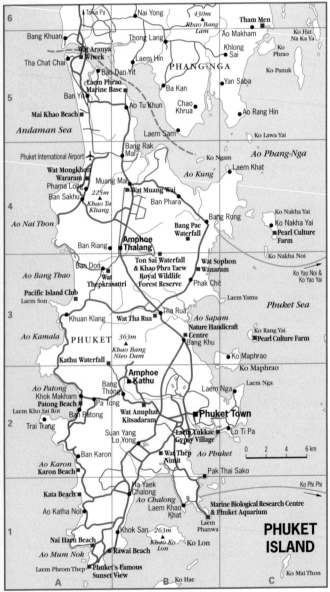

PHUKET ISLAND

Takua Pa • Nai Yong • 430m
▲ *Khao Bang Lam*
Tham Men ■
Bang Khuan • Ko Hat Na Ka Ya
Thong Lang • Ao Makham
Wat Aranya Wiwek Khlong Sai Ko Phrao
Tha Chat Chai • Laem Hin PHANG-NGA
Ban Dan Yit • Ko Panuk
Laem Phrao Marine Base ■ Ba Kan Yan Saba •
Ban Yit •
Ao Tu Khun • Chao Khrua Ao Rang Hin •
Mai Khao Beach ■
Andaman Sea Laem Sam •
Bang Rak Mai • Ko Ngam Laem Khat •
Phuket International Airport *Ao Phang-Nga*
Wat Mongkhon Wararam Ao Kung
Phana Long Muang Mai • ■**Wat Muang Wai** Ko Nakha Yai
Ban Sakhu • 225m Ban Phara Ko Nakha Yai
Khao Ta Kliang Bang Rong **Pearl Culture Farm** ■
Ao Nai Thon Ban Riang • **Bang Pae Waterfall** ■
Ko Nakha Noi
Amphoe Thalang ● Ko Yao Noi & Ko Yao Yai
Ban Don • **Ton Sai Waterfall & Khao Phra Taew Royal Wildlife Forest Reserve** **Wat Sophon Wanaram** ■
Ao Bang Thao **Wat Thepkrasattri** Phak Chit • *Phuket Sea*
Pacific Island Club ■ Laem Yamu •
Laem Son Tha Rua • *Ao Sapam*
Khuan Klang • Wat Tha Rua **Nature Handicraft Centre** ■ Ko Rang Yai
PHUKET 363m Bang Khu • **Pearl Culture Farm** ■
Ao Kamala ▲ *Khao Bang Nieo Dam*
Kathu Waterfall ■ • Ko Maphrao
Amphoe Kathu ● Ko Maphrao
Ao Patong Bang Thong • Laem Nga • Laem Nga
Khok Makham Pa Tong
Patong Beach ■ **Wat Anuphat Kitsadaram** ■ **Phuket Town** ■
Laem Kho Sai Rot Ban Patong
Trai Trang ■ Suan Yang **Laem Tukkae Gypsy Village** Lo Ti Pa •
Lo Yong
Ban Karon • **Wat Thep Nimit** ■ *Ao Phuket*
Ao Karon 0 2 4 6 km
Karon Beach ■ Pak Thai Sako •
Kata Beach ■ Ha Yaek Chalong Ko Phi Phi
Ao Katha Noi • *Ao Chalong* Laem Khao Khat **Marine Biological Research Centre & Phuket Aquarium**
Khok San • 263m Laem Phanwa
Nai Harn Beach ■ ▲ *Khao Ko Lon* Ko Lon
Ao Mum Nok **Rawai Beach** ■
Laem Phrom Thep ■**Phuket's Famous Sunset View** Ko Hae • Ko Mai Thon

Phuket

The island of Phuket lies in the Andaman Sea just off the coast of Phang-nga Province and is joined to the mainland by a short causeway. At 810sq km, it is Thailand's largest island and has developed in the last 25 years into one of the most luxurious and elaborate beach resorts in the whole of Southeast Asia. The name Phuket derives from the Malay word *bukit* (hill) and is pronounced 'Pooket'.

In past centuries, Phuket was an important entrepôt on the eastern shore of the Bay of Bengal, handling shipping and dealing with sailors from the Arab and Malay worlds, India, Burma, China and, of course, Siam. By the 16th century, it was also well known to Europeans, as first Portuguese and Dutch, then English and French, sailed there.

Phuket enjoyed an unprecedented surge in wealth when tin was found in large quantities just offshore. Miners and businessmen arrived from the provinces of south China, adding a considerable Sinitic element to the island's already mixed population.

It was not until about 1975 that Phuket's potential for tourism was finally realised. Although more expensive than almost any other resort in Thailand, it is still reasonable by international standards, especially in view of its beauty and amenities.

What to See on and around Phuket

BEACHES ✪✪✪

Phuket is all about beaches – it has some of the best in the world. Nearly all the major ones are on the western shore of the island, running from Mai Khao in the north to Nai Harn in the south. The best known is Patong, which has developed a lively night-time scene not unlike that of Pattaya. Then there are more sedate beaches like Kata and Karon. All share Phuket's wonderful coastline on the Andaman Sea, offer excellent accommodation and food and make the perfect place for a beach-based holiday. There are fewer beaches on the island's east coast, but just beyond the southern tip of the island at Cape Phrom Thep – famous for its legendary sunsets – Rawai Beach deserves a mention.

DID YOU KNOW?

Thais set considerable store by a value they call *jai yen* or 'cool heart'. Difficult or compromising situations are best resolved by keeping cool and never by shouting or displays of bad temper, which will only worsen matters

---

Relaxing on the beach at Kata Noi, on the west coast of Phuket Island

---

🚌 54A2,56

✉ Phuket Island, 862km south of Bangkok

🍴 Excellent restaurants

🚐 *Songthaews* and *tuk-tuks* run to all beaches from Phuket Town

✈ Phuket International Airport

❓ Vegetarian Festival, Phuket Town, late Sep

57

+ 54A2
⊠ Andaman Sea, 40km
  south of Krabi
🍴 Good cafés in Ton Sai
  Village
🚢 Ferries from Krabi and
  Phuket

PHI PHI MARINE NATIONAL PARK ✪✪✪

Usually referred to as Phi Phi Island, this marine park actually consists of two islands, Phi Phi Don and Phi Phi Leh. Located equidistantly from Phuket and Krabi, they can be reached in about two hours. It is possible to stay in bungalow accommodation or, increasingly, trendy hotels on Phi Phi Don. There is no accommodation on Phi Phi Leh. Famous for their clear waters, coral reefs and white, sandy beaches (setting for the Leonardo DiCaprio film *The Beach*), the islands remain remarkably lovely despite ill-controlled development.

+ 56B2
⊠ Sea Gypsy Village east of
  Phuket Town at Laem
  Tukkae
🍴 Gypsy World Seafood
  Restaurant
🚐 *Songthaew* or *tuk-tuk*

SEA GYPSIES ✪

Phuket, with the islands of the Mergui Archipelago stretching north into Myanmar (Burma), is home to an unusual indigenous people: the *chao thalae* or 'people of

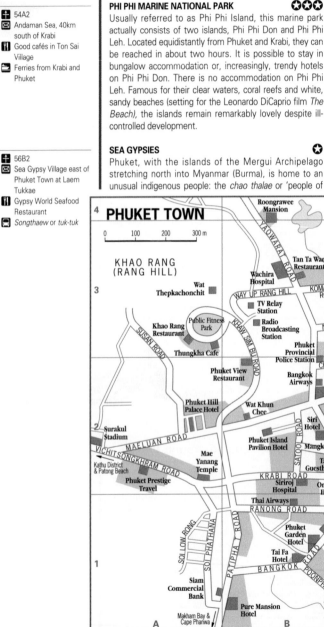

PHUKET TOWN

0   100   200   300 m

KHAO RANG
(RANG HILL)

Wat
Thepkachonchit

Public Fitness
Park

Khao Rang
Restaurant

Thungkha Cafe

WAY UP RANG HILL

Roongrawee
Mansion

Tan Ta Wan
Restaurant

Manor
Hotel

Wachira
Hospital

KOMARAPAT
ROAD

TV Relay
Station

Radio
Broadcasting
Station

NAKHON
ROAD

Phuket
Provincial
Police Station

CHUMPON
ROAD

Phuket View
Restaurant

Bangkok
Airways

Phuket
Merlin
Hotel

Phuket Hill
Palace Hotel

Wat Khun
Chee

Siri
Hotel

Wat
Mangkolnimit

Surakul
Stadium

Phuket Island
Pavilion Hotel

Talang
Guesthouse

MAELUAN ROAD

VICHITSONGKHRAM ROAD

Kathu District
& Patong Beach

Mae
Yanang
Temple

KRABI ROAD

Siriroj
Hospital

On-On
Hotel

Phuket Prestige
Travel

Thai Airways

RANONG ROAD

SOI PHATHANA

Phuket
Garden
Hotel

Post
Office

Tai Fa
Hotel

BANGKOK ROAD

Koh
Sawan
Hotel

Siam
Commercial
Bank

Makham Bay &
Cape Phanwa

Pure Mansion
Hotel

A   B

the sea', often called 'sea gypsies'. Now reduced to a tiny minority of the Phuket population, they traditionally make their living from the sea, spending most of their lives in boats. Their village is on Laem Tukkae.

Snorkelling and boating are popular activities at Phi Phi Leh

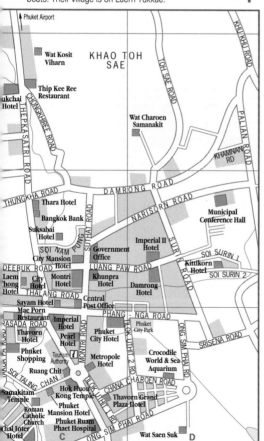

59

Old Phuket Town

Distance
2km

Time
1–2 hours

Start point
Central Post Office, Montri Road
 59C2
Songthaew

End point
Government Office
59C2

Lunch
Raan Jee Nguat (£)
Corner of Yaowarat and Deebuk Roads

Phuket town is a traditional meeting place of Thai and Malay worlds. Add to this a long association with European seafaring nations such as Portugal, Holland, France and Great Britain, plus an established tradition of ethnic Chinese settlement, mainly from Fujian Province, and the result is a heady cultural mix perhaps best exemplified by Phuket's Sino-Portuguese architecture.

During the latter part of the 19th century, a Sino-Thai businessman called Kor-Sim-Bi Na Ranong was appointed Governor of Phuket. Together with other affluent Chinese settlers he supervised the construction of richly decorated hybrid mansions, combining arched windows and doors with Doric, Ionic and Corinthian supporting columns.

Start at the Central Post Office. Walk west along Thalang Road, noting the Standard Chartered Bank building, turn south along Yaowarat Road to Fountain Circle. Head west once more along Ranong Road, noting the Thai Airways building, a fine example of Sino–Portuguese architecture.

Characteristic Sino-Portuguese architecture in Phuket Town

While intricate European neo-classical and Renaissance-style stucco designs grace the façades of the shophouses, the furnishings and atmosphere within are more Straits Chinese than European.

At the west end of Ranong Road turn north along Patiphat Road, then east along historic Krabi Road to return to Thalang Road. If you have the energy, turn left at the end of Thalang Road and head north along Suthat Road. On the right, just after the junction with Luang Paw Road and Deebuk Road, is the Sala Phuket or Government Office, an interesting example of colonial architecture.

What to See in Southern Thailand

ANG THONG NATIONAL MARINE PARK ✪✪

Comprising 40 small islands, Ang Thong is a spectacular combination of karst outcrops, azure lagoons, perfect beaches and swaying coconut palms. The tiny archipelago is uninhabited and best visited as a day trip from Ko Samui. Climb to the top of the most accessible peak (240m) and marvel at the spectacular natural beauty around you.

CHA-AM ✪

This small, friendly town is a popular weekend destination for people living in Bangkok. It has a long beach lined with casuarina trees, excellent seafood (as throughout the peninsular south) and a wide choice of accommodation. Cha-Am can get pretty busy at weekends, particularly during school holidays, but the beach is generally quiet on weekdays.

HUA HIN ✪

Hua Hin, just 25km south of Cha-Am, is the antithesis of Pattaya, its brash sister resort on the opposite side of the Bight of Bangkok. This trendy, family-orientated destination is Thailand's oldest beach resort. King Rama VII built a palace called Glai Gangwon or 'Far from Cares' there in 1928. Hua Hin is also well known for its renowned Hua Hin Railway Hotel, a fine colonial building renamed Hotel Sofitel Central.

KHAO SOK NATIONAL PARK (➤ 20, TOP TEN)

KO PHA-NGAN ✪✪

The second largest island in the Samui archipelago, Ko Pha-Ngan lies about half an hour's ferry ride north of Samui, and is much less developed – though this is changing fast. Because it is cheaper than Samui, Pha-Ngan draws more budget visitors and fewer high-rollers. Like Samui, the island has numerous fine beaches, a densely wooded and mountainous interior and several beautiful waterfalls. It has no 'capital' to speak of – the main town and port at Thong Sala is tiny. Most visitors head to the beaches and stay in bungalows, although hotels and more upmarket accommodation are available.

Wooden fishing boats at Cha-am

☐ 54B4
✉ 31km northwest of Ko Samui
⛴ Ferries from Ko Samui

☐ 40B2
✉ 180km south of Bangkok
🚌 Buses from Bangkok
🚉 Cha-Am Station
🛣 Phetkasem Highway
☎ (032) 471005

☐ 54B6
✉ 205km south of Bangkok
🍴 Railway Restaurant (£££)
🚌 Buses from Bangkok
🚉 Direct from Hualamphong Station, Bangkok
ℹ Municipal Office, Phetkasem Road
☎ (032) 511047
↔ Khao Sam Roi Yot National Park

☐ 63B5
✉ 15km north of Ko Samui, Gulf of Thailand
🚌 Regular air-conditioned buses from Bangkok to Surat Thani
🚉 Surat Thani
⛴ Night ferry from Ban Don, boats from Ko Samui
✈ Regular flights from Bangkok to Ko Samui Airport

61

KO SAMUI ✪✪✪

The Samui archipelago became a budget visitor's paradise back in the 1970s, but has since become considerably smarter. The main island of the group, Ko Samui, is Thailand's premier beach resort along with Phuket. There is not much to do at Nathon, the main town and port for arrival by ferry. The chief seaside destinations are Chaweng Beach on the island's east coast and Lamai on the south coast. The island is ringed by a well-maintained road, and the hilly interior is packed with coconut trees. Ko Samui can be reached by ferry from Surat Thani or by air from Bangkok. There are more than 10 flights a day from the Thai capital, which gives some indication of the popularity and appeal of this lovely island.

KO TAO ✪

Ko Tao (Turtle Island) is the most northerly and least developed destination in the Samui archipelago. Like its sister islands, the main industries are fishing, coconut farming and, increasingly, tourism. Since it takes several hours to reach the island from the mainland, most visitors stay for several days. It is an ideal place to lie back and relax, with good swimming, diving and snorkelling, as well as the cheapest accommodation in the group.

KRABI ✪✪

This fast-developing provincial capital is known for eco-tourism. Local agencies arrange half-day trips to mangrove swamps, visits to the nearby Khao Nor Chuchi rainforest and sea-kayaking trips along the Andaman coast. The best beaches are out of the town, which is located on a riverine estuary. For excellent swimming and sunbathing, try Hat Ton Sai, Hat Rai Leh and Hat Tham Phra Nang, all fine beaches easily reached by boat. Krabi also has regular ferry services to Phi Phi Island (➤ 58).

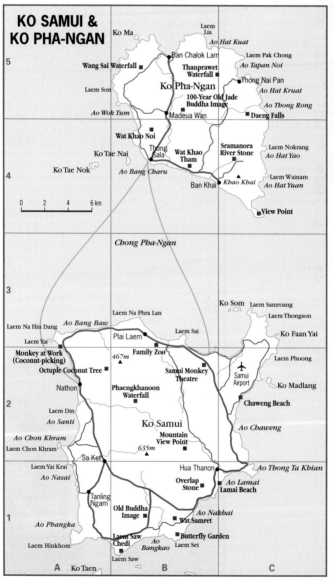

KO SAMUI & KO PHA-NGAN

5

Ko Ma

Laem Lia

Ao Hat Kuat

Laem Pak Chong

Ban Chalok Lam

Wang Sai Waterfall ■

Thanprawet Waterfall ■

Ao Tapan Noi

Thong Nai Pan ●

Ao Hat Kruat

Ko Pha-Ngan

Laem Son

100-Year Old Jade Buddha Image

Ao Thong Rong

Ao Wok Tum

● Madeua Wan

Daeng Falls ■

Wat Khao Noi ■

Thong Sala

Wat Khao Tham

Sramanora River Stone

Laem Nokrang

Ao Hat Yao

Ko Tae Nai

Ko Tae Nok

Ao Bang Charu

Laem Wainam

Ao Hat Yuan

4

Ban Khai ▲ *Khao Khai*

View Point ■

0   2   4   6 km

Chong Pha-Ngan

3

Ko Som   Laem Samroang

Laem Thongson

Laem Na Phra Lan

Laem Na Hin Dang   *Ao Bang Baw*

Laem Sai

● Ko Faan Yai

Laem Yai

Plai Laem ■

Monkey at Work (Coconut-picking) ■

467m ▲

Family Zoo ■

Laem Phoong

Octuple Coconut Tree ■

Samui Monkey Theatre ■

Samui Airport ✈

Nathon ●

Phaengkhanoon Waterfall ■

Ko Madlang

Laem Din

Ko Samui

Chaweng Beach ■

Ao Santi

2

Ao Chon Khram

Mountain View Point ■

Ao Chaweng

Laem Chon Khram

635m ▲

Laem Yai Krai

Sa Ket ●

Hua Thanon ●

Ao Thong Ta Khian

Ao Nasai

Overlap Stone ■

Ao Lamai

Lamai Beach ■

Tanling Ngam

Old Buddha Image ■

Ao Nakhai

1

Wat Samret ■

Ao Phangka

Laem Saw Chedi ■

Ao Bangkao

Butterfly Garden ■

Laem Set

Laem Hinkhom

Laem Saw

A   Ko Taen   **B**   **C**

63

➕ 54B3
✉ 780km south of Bangkok
🍴 Tamnak Thai (££)
🚌 Buses from Bangkok
🚉 Nakhon Si Thammarat
✈ 5km north of town
ℹ Off Thanon
Ratchadamnoen
☎ (075) 346515
♿ Few
❓ Chak Phra Pak Tai
festival, Wat Phra
Mahathat, mid-Oct

➕ 54C1
✉ 1,150km south of
Bangkok
🍴 Food stalls serving
southern curries (£)
🚌 Regular air-conditioned
buses from Bangkok
✈ Narathiwat Airport, links
from Bangkok and Phuket
♿ None
❓ Narathiwat Fair, last
week of Sep

➕ 54C1
✉ 1,055km south of
Bangkok
🚌 Regular air-conditioned
buses from Bangkok
✈ Hat Yai Airport, 110km
away with bus service
provided
♿ None
❓ Chao Mae Lim Ko Niao
Fair, Feb

NAKHON SI THAMMARAT ★

In many ways Nakhon Si Thammarat, although smaller than Hat Yai, is the real capital of the south. Relatively few tourists visit this historic city, despite the fact that the remains of the old city walls and some of the temples – notably the magnificent Wat Phra Mahathat – are well worth seeing. There are quite a few mosques, too, a sure sign of the south, although most Muslims here speak Thai not Malay. Just to the north of town is a lovely, casuarina-lined beach called Hat Sa Bua. It can be crowded at weekends but makes a great retreat, complete with excellent seafood restaurants, on ordinary weekdays.

NARATHIWAT ★

The capital of the southernmost province in Thailand, Narathiwat is famous for its mangoes and songbirds. The people are almost exclusively Malay-speaking Muslims (though Thai nationals) and this is reflected in the food and general culture. Most officials are Thai and the commercial district is dominated by ethnic Chinese; otherwise it is almost as if you had crossed the border into Malaysia. The usual Gulf formula applies – quiet, clean beaches, excellent seafood and friendly people – but, because of its distance from Bangkok, there are few tourists.

PATTANI ★

Like Narathiwat, Pattani is overwhelmingly populated by Malay-speaking Muslims, although it has an influential ethnic Chinese community. Pattani is an important fishing port, once capital of an independent (if small) kingdom, and memories of its independence still linger in local minds. There is plenty of accommodation but only one beach – Laem Tachi, 10km long, to the north.

Central Mosque, Pattani

PHANG-NGA BAY (➤ 22, TOP TEN)

PRACHUAP KHIRI KHAN ✪

About 80km down the Gulf coast, the small town of Prachuap Khiri Khan is far enough from Bangkok to discourage day-trippers and even weekenders. There are fine beaches to the north and the south of town; the latter, at Ao Prachuap, is 8km long and very pretty. An interesting side trip is a visit to Ao Bang Nang Lom, just north of Ao Prachuap, where wooden fishing boats are still made in the traditional way. Visitors may also climb Khao Chong Krajok or 'mirror mountain' for a fine view of the town and bay.

✚	54B5
✉	285km south of Bangkok
🍴	Pan Phochana (££)
🚍	Regular air-conditioned buses from Bangkok
🚆	Direct links from Hualamphong Station, Bangkok
♿	Few
↔	Wat Khao Tham Khan Kradai, cave temple ✉ 8km north of Hua Hin

RANONG ✪

The town of Ranong, near the banks of the Pakchan River, is not very interesting in itself but makes an ideal base for visiting the nearby Myanmar town of Kawthaung, better known as Victoria Point. This can be done in a day trip. Regular boats leave the pier on the Thai side of the river. Currently it costs US$5 for a day pass to enter Myanmar (the modern name for Burma).

✚	54A4
✉	645km south of Bangkok
🍴	Palm Court (££)
🚍	Regular air-conditioned buses from Bangkok
✈	Ranong Airport, 20km south of town
♿	None

SONGKHLA ✪

An attractive beach resort, Songkhla is a quietly cultured place. Apart from its fascinating national museum in a century-old Sino-Portuguese-style building, it boasts Songkhla Nakarin, the most prestigious university in southern Thailand, several colleges and, on nearby Ko Yo (Yo Island), the Institute of Southern Thai Studies. Southern Thai cuisine is almost always excellent but Songkhla is famed particularly for its seafood. For those interested in wildlife, Khukhut Waterbird Sanctuary is 30km north of town.

✚	54B2
✉	950km south of Bangkok
🍴	Excellent seafood restaurants
🚍	Regular air-conditioned buses from Bangkok
🚆	Hat Yai Station, 26km taxi ride to Songkhla
✈	Hat Yai Airport, taxi to Songkhla
♿	Few

Prow of a fishing vessel drawn up on the beach, Songkhla

65

Northern Thailand

Northern Thailand has a different atmosphere to the rest of the kingdom. This is because the region did not come under the full control of Bangkok until the first decade of the 20th century. For several hundred years it existed as an independent state called Lan Na, or the 'Kingdom of a Million Rice Fields'. The traditions and language of the north developed independently from those of central Thailand. Its people even used to dress differently; the women wearing their hair long in contrast to the cropped locks of their Siamese counterparts, the men covering their bodies with intricate tattoos to ward off sickness and injury.

Diversions for visitors, too, are very different, from whitewater rafting to trekking on foot or elephant, while the cities, especially Chiang Mai, have perhaps the nation's loveliest temples. This land of forested mountains and lush valleys is populated by sophisticated Buddhist lowlanders and a wide range of hill tribes.

'This country…if not the promised land, is yet one which grows dearer to the heart the more one knows it, and makes the stranger feel that…he could not find a land of greater charm and sympathy.'

REGINALD LE MAY, *(on Northern Thailand)*
An Asian Arcady (1926)

Left: *Wat Phrathat Doi Suthep*

Chiang Mai

Founded seven centuries ago by King Mangrai the Great, Chiang Mai has remained the political and cultural heart of the north from the time of the independent Lan Na kingdom to the present. Lan Na passed through a golden age in the 14th and 15th centuries but in 1558 was conquered by the Burmese and became a vassal state. It was not until 1775 that Lord Kavila, the ruler of Lampang, the second largest city of the north, drove out the Burmese. By this time Chiang Mai was all but depopulated and tigers roamed at will within the deserted fortifications.

Kavila gave orders for the city to be abandoned completely between 1776 and 1796. In the latter year he resettled the city, pronounced it his new capital, and began to restore the fortifications. The bastions, moats and remains of the city walls that contribute so much to the city's beauty date from this time. Over the next century Chiang Mai and the north became increasingly tied to Bangkok, and in 1932 the last vestiges of northern independence disappeared

Novice monk at a Chiang Mai temple

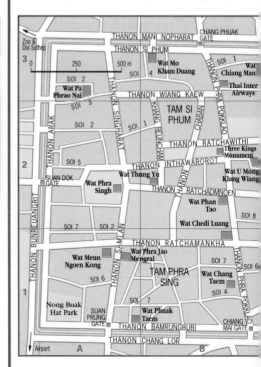

when the region became a province of Thailand.

Taking a trishaw or three-wheeled bicycle/taxi in Chiang Mai

As the north becomes more prosperous and the government in Bangkok increasingly confident and secure, northerners have begun to reassert their culture. The heart of this movement and the acknowledged capital of the region is Chiang Mai, dubbed 'the Rose of the North'. The city has much to offer the visitor, from temples and historic monuments to fine restaurants and golden sunsets accentuated by Doi Suthep, its guardian mountain.

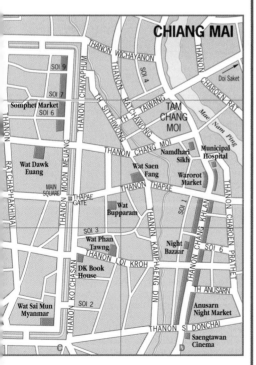

CHIANG MAI

Two visitors admiring a huge bronze bell at Wat Phra That Doi Suthep

What to See in and around Chiang Mai

BAW SANG UMBRELLA VILLAGE ⊕⊕

This village is devoted to the manufacture and sale of painted and lacquered paper umbrellas. Almost every household seems to be involved in the business. Visitors can visit the many workshops to see how the umbrellas are made and are welcome to take photos. Fans, silverware, bamboo and teak furniture, celadon and lacquerware are also made. There is even a local Muslim family making fans decorated with verses from the Koran.

✚ 74B3
✉ Route 1006, 9km east of Chiang Mai
🕐 Daily 7–5:30
🍴 On main street
🚌 *Songthaew* or *tuk-tuk*
♿ Few
✋ Free
❓ Umbrella Festival, Jan

Decorating umbrellas at Baw Sang Village

DOI INTHANON (► 17, TOP TEN)

DOI SUTHEP ⊕⊕⊕

The mountain dominating Chiang Mai to the west has two peaks, Doi Suthep and Doi Pui, which together constitute a national park. The road to the summit leads past several waterfalls, most notably – about 7km from town – the Monthatharn Falls, a picnic spot. At the 14km road marker, about two-thirds of the way up, is the beautiful and much revered Wat Phrathat Doi Suthep. This temple, easily seen from Chiang Mai, provides wonderful views across the valley. Nearer the summit, the gardens of Phuping Palace can be a riot of colour from November to February.

✚ 74B3
✉ 16km west of Chiang Mai
🕐 Temple Daily 6–6; Palace Gardens Sat–Sun 8:30–12:30, 1–4 (closed when royal family in residence)
🍴 Cafés near the temple (£)
🚌 *Songthaews* from front of Chiang Mai University, Thanon Huay Kaew
♿ None

LAMPANG ⊕

The only city in Thailand that continues to use pony carts for transport (now mainly for sightseeing), Lampang is an hour's drive south of Chiang Mai. The north's second largest city prospered as a teak town in the 19th century when merchants moved there from Myanmar (Burma). Burmese influence is visible in the city's temples, at least four of which have Burmese abbots. The oldest part of town, with the most historic monuments, lies to the north of the River Wang, which runs through the city.

✚ 74B3
✉ 92km south of Chiang Mai
🍴 Riverside Bar and Restaurant (££)
🚌 Buses from Bangkok
🚆 Lampang Station
✈ Lampang Airport
♿ Few
❓ Elephant Satok Fair, Feb

Old Chiang Mai

One of the great attractions of Chiang Mai, especially of the Old City, are the numerous back lanes or *soi*. Quiet and shaded, they offer the visitor a unique chance to observe contemporary Thai urban life as they wind back and forth between the busier main streets of the city.

The best place to begin a walk around the Old City is Thapae Gate. Start here and walk west along Thanon Ratchadamnoen before turning south along Thanon Phra Pokklao.

On the right you will pass a fine 19th-century wooden temple called Wat Phan Tao. Once part of the royal palace of the rulers of Chiang Mai, the building was reconsecrated as a temple in 1876. Shortly beyond, it is impossible to miss the large gateway opening onto Wat Chedi Luang. King Saen Meuang Ma of Lan Na founded the great *chedi* (pagoda) of this temple in the late 14th century. In its present restored form it is about 60m high but before an earthquake damaged it in 1545 the central spire was almost 90m. The compound also houses the city pillar.

Continue west through the temple grounds, turn north along Thanon Chaban and then west again when you rejoin Thanon Ratchadamnoen.

In the distance, against Doi Suthep, you will see Wat Phra Singh, the city's most important and revered temple, founded about 1350. Note the elegant raised library building decorated with stucco angels; also the classical murals of the restored Viharn Laikhram.

Leave by the main gateway and head north to the cross-roads; turn east along Thanon Inthawarorot to the Three Kings Monument, built to commemorate the founding of the city. Return to the Thapae Gate area by any of the narrow lanes heading east.

Distance
2.5km

Time
2–3 hours, depending on temple visits

Start point
Thapae Gate
✚ 69C2
🚐 *Songthaew* or *tuk-tuk*

End point
The Three Kings Monument
✚ 68B2

Lunch
Sri Pen (£)
✉ Thanon Inthawarorot, just off Thanon Singharat

The old temple of Wat Phra Singh

74B3
 26km south of Chiang Mai
Regular buses from Chiang Mai
None
Longan Fair, Aug

Lamphun's distinguished Wat Phra That Haripunchai

LAMPHUN: WAT PHRA THAT HARIPUNCHAI ✪✪

Just 30 minutes' drive south of Chiang Mai, Lamphun was founded in AD 950 and is the oldest continually inhabited city in Thailand. The old Chiang Mai–Lamphun road is lined for several kilometres with 30m-high ancient yang trees. Dating from 1467, the stepped pyramid-shaped Suwanna *chedi* (pagoda) of the beautiful Wat Phra That Haripunchai is one of the few examples of Dvaravati Mon architecture surviving in Thailand. Nearby hangs a giant gong, reputed to be the largest in the world. Opposite the temple is the excellent Lamphun National Museum.

 69D1
Thanon Chang Khlan, Chiang Mai
Daily 5–11
Bars and cafés down each edge of the bazaar
Songthaews
Few
Free

NIGHT BAZAAR ✪✪✪

Located in the heart of downtown Chiang Mai, this bustling, three-storey market sells every variety of hill-tribe craft, antique, pseudo-antique and souvenir, all at very reasonable prices and difficult to beat elsewhere. It is necessary to bargain, however. In addition to the night bazaar building there is a busy street market all along central Thanon Chang Khlan.

WAT PHRA THAT LAMPANG LUANG (► 26, TOP TEN)

Outside Chiang Mai

This drive forms part of an 80km loop encircling the Doi Suthep–Doi Pui National Park, returning to Chiang Mai via the small settlement of Samoeng.

Thirteen kilometres north of Chiang Mai, just beyond the market town of Mae Rim, a well-signposted road leads west into the hills through the lush and beautiful Mae Sa Valley.

The 'Samoeng Loop' via Mae Sa makes a fine day's outing featuring magnificent scenery, ample diversions and attractions, good food and a well-maintained road.

At the start of the Mae Sa Valley there is a snake farm (where cobras are milked for production of anti-venom) and a butterfly farm, filled with gorgeous and often huge specimens. The road continues past an elephant training centre where visitors can watch the great beasts being put through their paces and enjoy a ride on elephant back. Drive west on route 1096 and after 13km you will find the Queen Sirikit Botanical Gardens, a treasure house of flora created with the assistance of Kew Gardens in England. Beyond the gardens the road climbs high into the hills, winding backwards and forwards in a series of great loops that afford fine views westward over the mountains toward Myanmar (Burma).

Elephants and their trainers taking a bath in the river

Stop for lunch in Samoeng or bypass the town altogether.

The road back to Chiang Mai crosses the Krisda Doi Pass and runs by several attractive resorts amid magnificent scenery.

Distance
103km

Time
3 hours

Start/end point
Chiang Mai
➕ 74B3

Lunch
Samoeng Resort (£)
✉ 79 Moo 2, KM35, Mae Rim-Samoeng Road
☎ (053) 487074

Dancers at the annual Longan Fruit Fair, Lamphun

NORTHERN THAILAND

0   20   40   60   80 km

BUR

Baw Sang
Fang

Ban Na Wai

Huay Nam Dang
National Park

Mae Suya

1834m
Doi Khun
Huay Fang

Lum Nam Pai
Wildlife Sanctuary   Pai

Chiang Dao   Phrao

Mae Hong Son

Tang Dao Elephant
Training Centre

Muang Paeng
Hot Spring

Mae Taeng

Queen Sirikit
Botanical Gardens   Mae Sa Valley
Mae Rim

Nam Tok Mae Surin
National Park   Samoeng

Khun Yuam

Doi Suthep-Doi Pui
National Park

Ban Pong Din

Chiang Mai

Mae Yuam
Luang Waterfall

Huay Thong

Ob Khan
Nat Park   Bow Sang

CHIANG MAI

Lamphun

Doi Khun Tan
National Park

2600m
Doi Inthanon

MAE HONG SON   Mae Chaem

Tham Mae Hu

Doi Inthanon
National Park   LAMPHUN
Ban Hong

Lampang

Thappanom
Hot Spring

Wat Phra That
Lampang Luang

Mae Sariang   Hot

Ban Kiu Lom

Mae Tan

Mae Tub
Reservoir   Doi Tao

Sop Prap

Om Koi

Ko Waterfall

Mae Ping
National Park   Thoen

Ban Tha
Song Yang

Thung
Kwian

1666m
Doi Khui Liang   Bhumiphol
Reservoir

1027m
Doi Tha Chi

TAK

Mae
Ramat

Ton Krabak Yai
National Park

Somdet Phra
Jao Taksin
Maharat Shrine

Tak

BUR

Mae Sot   Lan Liang
Ma Waterfall

Khao Son
Forest Park

A   B

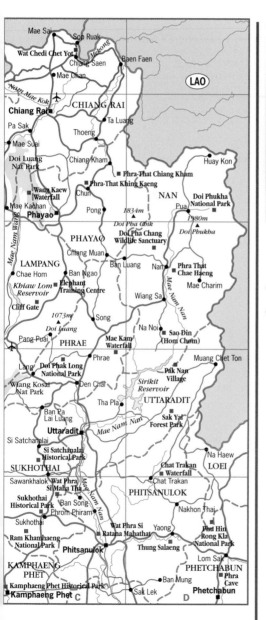

Motor-biking in the
northern hills

BUR Burma (Myanmar)

LAO Laos

What to See in Northern Thailand

CHIANG RAI

An excellent way to travel to Chiang Rai, 'Gateway to the Golden Triangle', is to overnight at one of the comfortable riverside lodges in Thaton, 180km north of Chiang Mai. Follow the river – fast by long-tail boat, or slow by raft – to Chiang Rai. It has little of historic interest but a lot in the way of tourist facilities and is the main base for exploring the Golden Triangle region, where the borders of Myanmar (Burma), Laos and Thailand come together.

75C4
100km north of Chiang Mai
Buses from Bangkok and Chiang Mai
Chiang Rai Airport
Thanon Singkhlai
☎ (053) 717433
Lychee Fair, May

CHIANG SAEN AND THE GOLDEN TRIANGLE

The historic town of Chiang Saen, dating from the 12th century, is on the west bank of the Mekong River about 90 minutes' drive from Chiang Rai. Here you can explore the town's ruins, take a boat trip or sit and enjoy a cool drink while gazing across the river into nearby Laos. Just 10km north of Chiang Saen, by road along the bank of the river, is Sop Ruak, the heart of the infamous 'Golden Triangle'. It is worth checking out the Opium Museum here – but not the real thing (you risk arrest and a heavy fine).

75C5
60km north of Chiang Rai
Border View (££)
Regular air-conditioned buses from Chiang Mai and Chiang Rai

Bamboo rafts with cabins on the Kok River at Chiang Rai

MAE HONG SON

Once one of Thailand's remotest provinces, Mae Hong Son is now readily accessible by air from Chiang Mai, as well as by a wonderful loop drive through Mae Sariang and back via Pai – or vice versa. Mae Hong Son is not yet very developed, but there are at least two quality resort hotels. Although Thai citizens, most of the townsfolk are of Shan, Karen, Yunnanese Chinese or hill-tribe descent. The temples are Burmese in style and the pace of life slow.

74A4
270km northwest of Chiang Mai going through Pai
Bai Fern (££)
Regular air-conditioned buses from Chiang Mai
Mae Hong Son Airport
Poi Sang Long, 1–3 Apr

MAE SAI

The chief attraction of this small commercial enclave on the banks of the Sai River, about 90 minutes' drive from Chiang Rai, is Myanmar (Burma). It is possible to make a day trip across the river without a visa – a US$5 charge applies at the border bridge – and stroll around the Myanmar border town of Thakhilek. The people are friendly and speak better English than the Thais but are palpably less well-off. By arrangement with a local tour office, visitors can also make a three-day round trip to Kengtung, the main city of the eastern Shan state of Myanmar.

NAN ✪

Until about 20 years ago Nan was considered 'unsafe' because of a smouldering communist insurgency in the province. It is still off the beaten track but quite safe to visit. This sleepy provincial capital, which only becomes busy in October and November when the annual dragon boat races are held, is remarkable for Wat Phumin, a temple rich in 19th-century murals painted by unknown artists that record scenes of secular and religious society in Nan 150 years ago.

75C5
65km north of Chiang Rai
Rabieng Kaew (££)
Regular air-conditioned buses from Chiang Rai, VIP bus to Bangkok

Typical accommodation at the Mae Hong Son Resort

75D3
318km east of Chiang Mai
Siam Pochana (£)
Regular air-conditioned buses from Bangkok and Chiang Mai
Nan Airport
Lanna Boat Races, Oct–Nov

77

Hotel Wang Yom, one of the few places to stay in Si Satchanalai

75C1

✉ 377km north of Bangkok

🍴 Excellent riverside restaurants

🚌 Buses from Bangkok

🚉 Phitsanulok Station

✈ Phitsanulok Airport, slightly south of town

ℹ 209/7–8 Thanon Borom Trailokanat
☎ (055) 252743

♿ Few

❓ Phitsanulok Boat Races, 16–17 Sep

75D1

✉ Park HQ 125km east of Phitsanulok

🍴 Vendors near the bungalows

🚌 Ordinary bus from Phitsanulok to Nakhon Thai, *songthaew* to park

♿ None

 Cheap

PHITSANULOK ✪

Phitsanulok is an excellent base for exploring the nearby historical sites at Sukhothai, Si Satchanalai, Sawankhalok and even Kamphaeng Phet. It has some of the best accommodation and restaurants in the lower north, the latter especially along the banks of the Nam River which snakes through the town. Wat Phra Si Ratana Mahathat is the most important temple in Phitsanulok. Its main hall contains the Phra Phuttha Chinnarat, symbol of the province and one of the most distinguished Buddha images in the kingdom. Cast in the late Sukhothai period, about six centuries ago, the golden, flame-haloed image is extremely elegant and highly venerated.

PHU HIN RONG KLA NATIONAL PARK ✪

Between 1967 and 1982, Phu Hin Rong Kla was the headquarters of Thailand's communist insurgents, engaged in a protracted guerrilla war with Thai government forces based in and around Phitsanulok. Today, a visit to the park makes a great day trip. The countryside *en route* is spectacular and visitors to the park can see the Red Flag Cliff, the former Communist Party of Thailand headquarters, and other reminders of the struggle.

DID YOU KNOW?

Kap Klaem or 'drinking food' is a name applied by Thais to snacks served as an accompaniment to alcoholic drinks. These snacks include peanuts, cashews, potato chips, pork rinds, shrimp cakes, sun-dried beef jerky and deep-fried grasshoppers and locusts.

SI SATCHANALAI ★★★

Si Satchanalai–Chaliang Historical Park is less visited than Sukhothai but, arguably, more attractive. Dating from the 11th century, the ruins are similar to those at Sukhothai, but less restored and less immaculately kept, adding a mystique to the atmosphere. If this early Thai kingdom fascinates you, be sure to visit the former kilns at Sawankhalok, midway between Sukhothai and Si Satchanalai. Further to the southwest the third ancient city of the Sukhothai kingdom, Kamphaeng Phet, is undergoing major restoration and is well worth a visit.

SUKHOTHAI HISTORICAL PARK (► 25, TOP TEN)

➕ 75C2
✉ 70km north of Sukhothai
🍴 Restaurants in nearby Sawankhalok
🚌 Regular air-conditioned buses from Sukhothai to park entrance

Wat Chang Lom, at Si Satchanalai

Food & Drink

Popular in the West for the past 20 years, Thai cuisine ranks beside French, Italian and Chinese as one of the most highly esteemed in the world. The good news is that Thai food is much more reasonably priced in Thailand than back home.

Rice

Rice is central to most Thai meals, although the national fondness for noodles shows the strength of Chinese influence. Thais eat two kinds of rice: slightly fluffy, long-grain rice, eaten with a spoon and fork, and 'sticky rice', eaten with the fingers. Noodles are always eaten with chopsticks.

Meat

Meat is generally stir-fried or otherwise cooked in bite-sized pieces, which explains the absence of knives on Thai tables. Thai pork is among the best in the world; chicken and duck are also excellent. Beef is widely available but can be a little tough. Consumption of lamb, mutton and goat is largely limited to Thailand's Muslim community.

Fish and Seafood

Fresh and saltwater fish, shrimp, lobsters, crabs, clams, mussels, squid and octopuses are all available. The best place to enjoy fresh seafood is by the sea but even Chiang Mai, amid the northern mountains, has excellent fresh seafood flown and trucked in daily. As Thailand has grown richer, so imported varieties of fish have become increasingly available; it is not surprising to find smoked salmon from Scotland or Norwegian herring on the menu.

Spicy dishes, sticky rice in bamboo and marinated duck all contribute to a sophisticated cuisine

Fruit and Vegetables

Fresh fruit and vegetables are available throughout the country, from temperate crops such as asparagus, celery, apples and strawberries grown in the cool north to more exotic varieties such as rambutan, mangosteen, durian, pineapple, mango and

tamarind that flourish in the warmer tropics. In recent years avocados have been introduced from Israel and kiwi fruit from New Zealand. Moreover, anything that does not grow in Thailand with ease – such as cherries, walnuts, nectarines and apricots – is flown in regularly and available on supermarket shelves or in restaurants.

Drink

Bottled, purified water and a wide range of internationally known soft drinks are available everywhere – even in remote places. Thailand produces several good (but strong) local brews including Singha (Lion) and Chang (Elephant) beers. International brands such as Carlsberg and Heineken are manufactured locally under licence. There is a plethora of local whiskies and rums and everything that can be imported is imported, from the best Russian vodka to the top Scotch malt. Thais have recently discovered a taste for wine, too, and import widely, although mainly from Australia.

Fresh fish and vegetables seasoned with chillies make delicious dishes

Mealtimes

Whatever, whenever. Thais eat when they are hungry and do not understand the Western concept of fixed mealtimes. They also tend to eat less than Westerners but more frequently. That said, all hotels and restaurants catering to foreign visitors are aware of the strange international habit of eating three fixed meals a day and make allowances for it.

Mang-khut or mangosteen

81

Isaan

Thailand's least-developed area, the great north-eastern region comprising the Khorat Plateau and Mekong Valley is worth visiting for its many attractions and the locals' engaging disposition. The people are Thai nationals whose mother tongue is Lao. They have a distinctive musical tradition and a spicy cuisine, loved by Thais. The Khorat Plateau is an immense, semi-arid tableland punctuated by the cities of Nakhon Ratchasima (also known as Khorat), Khon Kaen, Ubon Ratchathani and Udon Thani. The 'Khmer Culture Trail' – a jewel-like string of Khmer temples dating from the Angkor period – leads east from Nakhon Ratchasima to a point near Ubon Ratchathani.

The Mekong Valley is a lush region of green rice paddies, fishing villages and riverside market towns. Almost the entire west bank of the great river is driveable, and the influences of Vietnam, Cambodia and Laos are palpable in riverine settlements. Since 1994 the river has been bridged at Nong Khai by the Mittraphap or 'Friendship' Bridge, the main gateway to the nearby Lao capital of Vientiane.

'...the northeast is one of the most glorious, but least visited, destinations in Thailand.'

BEN DAVIES,
Adventure Traveller Southeast Asia (2000)

●

Left: *Prasat Hin Phanom Wan, near Nakhon Ratchasima*

What to See in Isaan

BAN CHIANG ✪

The small upper Isaan village of Ban Chiang is the site of one of the oldest known cultures in Southeast Asia. As early as 2000 BC people living in the vicinity were firing elegantly patterned clay pots. The location, now a UNESCO World Heritage Site, is worth visiting to see the excavations, Ban Chiang Museum and examples of the early bronze objects produced by Ban Chiang culture. The present inhabitants of Ban Chiang, although not necessarily related to the original potters, have taken up the trade with enthusiasm and produce attractive and

✚ 84B4
✉ 50km east of Udon Thani
🚌 Songthaew from Udon Thani

Museum
🕐 Daily 9–4
♿ Few
✋ Cheap

Rows of imitation Ban Chiang pots for sale

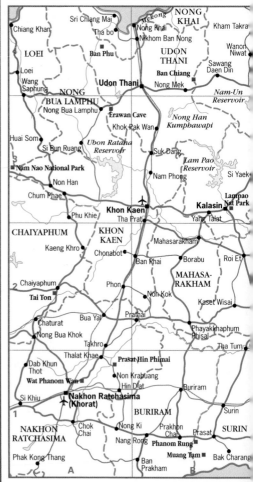

inexpensive imitations – but do not be tempted to buy the real thing as export is prohibited.

CHONABOT ✪

The small town of Chonabot is renowned for its weaving, particularly its *mat-mii* tie-dyed cotton and silk. A stroll almost anywhere in the village will lead past wooden houses raised on stilts, with local womenfolk weaving in the shade underneath. The best place to gain an overall impression of this upper Isaan art form is at the local handicraft centre on Thanon Pho Sii Sa-aat in the northern part of town. Here, in addition to silk and cotton cloth, ceramics and other assorted local handicrafts are for sale.

✚ 84A2
✉ 50km southwest of Khon Kaen
🕐 Centre: daily 9–6
🚌 *Songthaew* from Khon Kaen
❓ Silk Fair, Khon Kaen, 29 Nov–10 Dec

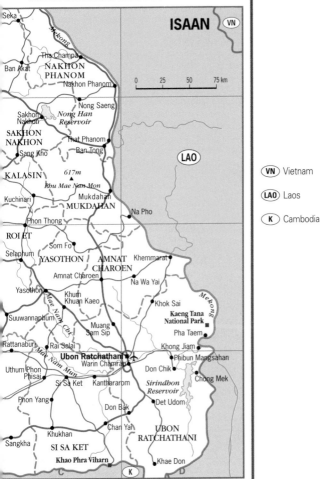

ISAAN — VN

VN Vietnam

LAO Laos

K Cambodia

🔲 85D1
✉ 75km east of Ubon Ratchathani
🍴 Food stalls at border post
🚌 Bus from Ubon to Phibun Mangsahan, *songthaew* from Phibun

The ruins of Khao Phra Viharn, a Khmer sanctuary

🔲 85C1
✉ 106km south of Si Sa Ket
🕐 Daily 6–6
🍴 Food stalls before Thai border point
🚌 *Songthaew* from Si Sa Ket
♿ None
🖐 Moderate

CHONG MEK AND THE EMERALD TRIANGLE ✪

The southeastern part of Isaan, around and beyond the Sirindhon Reservoir, is being quietly promoted by the Tourism Authority of Thailand as the 'Emerald Triangle', an Isaan equivalent to the 'Golden Triangle' of the north. Here, where the borders of Laos, Cambodia and Thailand meet, is some lovely unspoilt countryside including Kaeng Tana National Park. In August 2000 a new bridge across the Mekong river at Pakse was completed and the road via Chong Mek became the gateway to southern Laos.

KHAO PHRA VIHARN ✪✪

This massive, magnificent, 800-year-old Khmer temple, seated on a high escarpment of the Dongrek Mountains, lies across the frontier within Cambodian territory (where it is known as Preah Vihear) but is only accessible from Thailand. Visitors can cross into Cambodia without a visa by paying the 100 baht (about US$2.50) entry charge, leaving their passport and proceeding across the frontier on foot. It is a steep climb but worth it. The view across the Cambodian plain, about 200m below, is breathtaking.

Ubon Ratchathani

Ubon Ratchathani is the largest city in eastern Isaan and an important communications and agricultural centre. Located on the banks of the Mun River (pronounced 'moon'), it is really a twin city, with the railroad station and commercial centre of Warin Chamrap to the south of the river and Ubon proper to the north. There is little to see in Warin so a walk around Ubon should be limited to the north of the river. The Tourism Authority of Thailand office on Thanon Kheuan Thani has excellent free maps of the town.

Begin your walk at Wat Supatanaram in the southwestern part of Ubon by the banks of the Mun River.

Often shortened to Wat Supat, this interesting temple blends Khmer, Thai and Chinese styles. The *bot* or ordination hall is reminiscent of early Cambodian temples, being entirely of stone. The roof corners feature dragons rather than the usual 'sky hooks' associated with Thai temples. In front of the *bot* hangs the largest wooden bell in Thailand.

Head east from Wat Supat to the traffic circle, then north along Thanon Uparat – Ubon's main road – to turn right at the intersection with Thanon Kheuan Thani. Ubon National Museum is about 100m along on your left.

This is one of the best museums in Thailand. Look for the early Khmer exhibits and the 19th-century Ubon objects.

Walk east along Thanon Kheuan Thani. Turn north on Thanon Luang and proceed to Wat Thung Si Meuang on your left.

This temple, one of the oldest in Ubon, has 150-year-old murals based on the Buddha's life and a fine library which was built on stilts above a pool to discourage termites.

Distance
1.5km

Time
1–2 hours, depending on temple visits

Start point
Wat Supatanaram, Thanon Phromthep
✚ 85D1

End point
Wat Thung Si Meuang
✚ 85D1

Lunch
Chiokee (£)
✉ Thanon Kheuan Thani

Wax carving in the shape of a winged garuda (half bird, half man) at Ubon Ratchathani

85D2

74km east of Ubon Ratchathani

Floating restaurants on the Mun River

Ordinary buses from Ubon Ratchathani

None

KHONG JIAM ✪

This small settlement at the confluence of the Mun and Mekong rivers provides a quiet base for visitors wishing to explore the Emerald Triangle. Located on a picturesque peninsula between the two rivers, it is a good place for boating or fishing on the Mekong. Comfortable hotel and bungalow accommodation is available. About 20km north is the overhanging cliff of Pha Taem, featuring prehistoric paintings of people, fish, elephants and turtles estimated to be at least three millennia old. Views from the top of the cliff across the Mekong to Laos are spectacular.

84A1

250km northeast of Bangkok

Good Chinese restaurants

Buses from Bangkok

Nakhon Ratchasima

Nakhon Ratchasima

Few

Thao Suranari Festival, Mar–Apr

NAKHON RATCHASIMA ✪

The second largest city in Thailand, although much smaller than Bangkok, is the gateway to the northeast. Featuring good restaurants and accommodation, it is an ideal base for exploring Phimai. Mahawirawong National Museum has a good collection of early Khmer carvings and sculpture. In the middle of town stands a much-venerated shrine to Thao Suranari (also known as Khunying Mo), a local heroine who helped defeat a Lao invasion of Nakhon Ratchasima in the early 19th century.

84B4

620km northeast of Bangkok

Banya Pochana (££)

Regular air-conditioned buses from Bangkok

Nong Khai

Fresh fruit and vegetables at the evening market in Nakhon Ratchasima

NONG KHAI ✪

This pleasant riverside town is the jumping-off point for visits to nearby Laos, especially the Lao capital, Vientiane. Such visits had to be made by ferry until 1994, when the Mittraphap or 'Friendship' Bridge opened. Nong Khai is a quiet town with some attractive Sino-French architecture along Thanon Meechai. In the hot season (March to May), watch out for Phra That Klang Nam, 'the Holy Reliquary in the Midst of the River' – the remains of a Buddhist temple that slipped into the Mekong in 1850 and are visible only when the river runs at its lowest.

PRASAT PHANOM RUNG (► 23, TOP TEN)

The Mekong

The Mekong River (► 21) defines the frontier between Laos and Thailand for several hundred kilometres. A drive along the Mekong is exhilarating. The road follows the river from Chiang Khan in the north to Mukdahan in the east. Chiang Khan is a sleepy little riverside town with some fine restaurants overlooking the river.

From Chiang Khan drive east to Nong Khai, passing through a series of attractive Mekong Valley towns like Pak Chom and Sangkhom.

Sri Chiang Mai, opposite the Lao capital of Vientiane, is notable for its 'spring roll wrapper' production; note the thin discs of rice paste drying on rattan stands in the sun. Many of the inhabitants of Sri Chiang Mai are naturalised Thai citizens of Vietnamese origin – Vietnamese Catholic refugees crossed the Mekong in large numbers to escape the Communist authorities in Hanoi during the 1950s.

Beyond Nong Khai the road follows the Mekong in a long curve to the north and east before swinging south towards Nakhon Phanom.

There is little but open countryside and fine views of the wide river until you reach Nakhon Phanom, another city with a notable Vietnamese presence. This is a good place to stay overnight, with riverside restaurants offering views of the nearby, cone-shaped mountains of Laos.

About 105km further south, end your drive at tranquil Mukdahan, a ferry point for the border crossing to the Lao city of Savannakhet.

Distance
560km

Time
2 days

Start point
Chiang Khan
✚ 84A4

End point
Mukdahan
✚ 85C3

Lunch
Udom Rot (£)
✉ 423 Thanon Rim Khong, Nong Khai
☎ (042) 421084

Small passenger ferry crossing the mighty Mekong River to Laos

84A1

58km northeast of Nakhon Ratchasima

1305 from Nakhon Ratchasima

Historical Park daily 7:30–6

Few

Cheap

Phimai Long-Boat Races and Festival

84B1

452km northeast of Bangkok

Wang Petch (££)

Buses from Bangkok

Surin Station

85D1

630km northeast of Bangkok

Good Chinese and Vietnamese restaurants

Regular air-conditioned buses from Bangkok

Warin Chamrap Station

Ubon Ratchathani International Airport

Few

Central prang at Prasat Hin Phimai

PRASAT HIN PHIMAI
This remarkable Khmer temple was constructed in the late 10th to early 11th centuries as part of a network of Khmer religious structures connected with Angkor. Built of white and pink sandstone, the complex has been restored and, along with Phanom Rung, is one of the two finest Khmer temples outside Cambodia. The new Phimai National Museum, nearby, is highly recommended. There is also a vast banyan tree – looking more like a small forest than a single tree – where visitors can have their fortune told.

SURIN
For most of the year this quiet provincial capital lies off the beaten track. However, a carnival atmosphere pervades in November during the Surin Elephant Round-up, which is so popular that visitors must book in advance. Most of the local people, known as Suay, speak a variant of Khmer (as well as Thai) and are known for their skill with elephants.

UBON RATCHATHANI
Although one of Thailand's larger cities, Ubon Ratchathani is a long way from Bangkok and consequently rather off the tourist map. This is a pity, as it's an attractive, friendly, laid-back place that deserves more visitors. It is also a convenient base for exploring the Emerald Triangle, the Mekong River at Khong Jiam and Khao Phra Viharn.

Tucked away in the southeastern corner of lower Isaan, Ubon has long been defined as 'the end of the line' from Bangkok. This is changing, however, after the reopening of the ancient Khmer temple of Khao Phra Viharn just across the Cambodian border, and the completion of a new bridge across the Mekong at Pakse, in nearby Laos. Far from being the end of the line, Ubon is set to become the gateway to southern Laos and central Vietnam.

The city was home to an important US airbase during the Vietnam War but today is a quieter place, holding an annual candle festival in July and boasting a fine museum.

Where To...

Above: *musicians at the world famous Oriental Hotel in Bangkok*
Right: *a Thai child intent on his kite flying*

Central Thailand

Prices
Prices are approximate and include service but not drinks:

£ = under 200 baht
££ = 200–500 baht
£££ = over 500 baht

Licensing Laws
Virtually all restaurants in Thailand – unless they are Muslim – serve alcohol in the form of beer, spirits and, increasingly, wine, at any hour of the day. 'Licensing' – in the form of no alcoholic beverages for sale – only applies on holy days in the Buddhist calendar and during elections. In both these cases, special allowance is generally made for foreign visitors, who are not deemed likely to cause trouble during Thai elections.

Bangkok

Bei Otto (££)
Well-established German restaurant with *bierhaus*, delicatessen and bakery.
🗺 1 Sukhumvit Soi 20 ☎ (02) 262 0892 🕐 Lunch, dinner 🚇 E4 Asoke Station 🚌 1, 8, 11, 13, 38

Bourbon Street (££)
Cajun-Creole cookery (red beans and rice, gumbo, jambalaya). Mexican buffet on Tuesday nights.
🗺 Washington Square, Sukhumvit Soi 22 ☎ (02) 259 0328 🕐 Breakfast, lunch, dinner 🚇 E5 Phrom Phong Station 🚌 1, 8, 11, 13, 38

Bussaracum (£££)
Royal Thai cuisine (recipes created for the Thai royal court) amid elegant décor.
🗺 139 Sethiwan Building, Thanon Pun ☎ (02) 266 6312 🕐 Lunch, dinner 🚇 Surasuk Station 🚌 2, 4,

Celadon (£££)
Fine Thai restaurant with dishes like chicken grilled in screwpine leaves.
🗺 The Sukhothai Hotel, 13/3 Thanon Sathorn Tai ☎ (02) 287 0222 🕐 Lunch, dinner 🚌 17, 22, 62

Gianni's (££)
Simple, excellent Italian dishes such as angel-hair pasta with lobster. Two- and three-course set lunches.
🗺 34/1 Soi Tonson, Thanon Ploenchit ☎ (02) 252 1619 🕐 Lunch, dinner. Closed Sun 🚇 E2 Ploenchit Station 🚌 1, 8

Huntsman (££)
British-style pub serving popular dishes such as steak and kidney pie. Beef buffet on Monday evenings.

🗺 The Landmark Hotel, 138 Thanon Sukhumvit ☎ (02) 254 0404 🕐 Lunch, dinner 🚇 E3 Nana Station 🚌 1, 8, 11, 13, 38

Le Bistrot (£££)
The best French cuisine in Bangkok – worth every baht.
🗺 20/17-9 Soi Ruam Rudi ☎ (02) 251 2523 🕐 Lunch, dinner 🚇 E2 Ploenchit Station 🚌 1, 8

Lemongrass (££)
Excellent central Thai food (such as southern-style sweet and spicy grilled chicken) served in a fine old wooden house.
🗺 5/1 Soi 24 Thanon Sukhumvit ☎ (02) 258 8637 🕐 Lunch, dinner 🚇 E5 Phrom Phong Station 🚌 1, 8, 11, 13, 38

Mahboonkrong Food Centre (£)
A large range of food stalls providing Thai and international food in a bustling atmosphere.
🗺 Mahboonkrong Shopping Centre, corner of Thanon Phayathai and Thanon Rama I 🕐 Daily 10–9 🚇 Siam Square

Scala Shark's Fin (£££)
Serves the best shark's fin soup in Bangkok, plus a range of other Chinese specials.
🗺 483–485 Thanon Yaowarat ☎ (02) 623 0183 🕐 Lunch, dinner 🚇 Mahboonkrong 🚌 4, 5

Spice Market (£££)
One of the best Thai restaurants in Bangkok, in a replica Thai spice shop.
🗺 The Regent Hotel, 155 Thanon Ratchadamri ☎ (02) 251 6127 🕐 Lunch, dinner 🚇 S1 Ratchadamri Station 🚌 4, 5

Ayuthaya

Chainam (£)

A good place for Western breakfasts, especially if you arrive early in Ayuthaya. Good Thai and Western food at reasonable prices.

✉ Thanon U Thong, opposite Chan Kasem Palace
☎ (035) 252013 🕐 Breakfast, lunch, dinner

Phae Krung Kao (££)

Floating on the Pa Sak River, this attractive restaurant specialises in seafood and Thai chicken and pork dishes. Chinese delicacies are also available.

✉ Moo 2 Thanon U Thong
☎ (035) 241555 🕐 Lunch, dinner

Chanthaburi

Chanthon Phochana (£)

Chanthaburi is renowned for its tasty noodle dishes such as crab fried with noodles, recommended at this low-key restaurant. Also serves a wide variety of Chinese food.

✉ 98/1 Thanon Benchamarachutit ☎ (039) 312340 🕐 Lunch, dinner

Kanchanaburi

Mae Nam (££)

This pleasant, large, floating restaurant specialises in fish and seafood. Meat and vegetarian dishes are also available. Live music at night.

✉ On the river at the end of Thanon Lak Muang ☎ (034) 512811 🕐 Lunch, dinner

Punnee Café and Bar (£)

Popular with expatriate residents, serving Western-style Thai food and Thai-style European dishes plus 'the coldest beer in town'.

✉ Thanon Ban Neua ☎ (034) 513503 🕐 Lunch, dinner

Lopburi

Fa–Tong Chinese/Thai Restaurant (££)

Top Thai and Chinese cuisine plus standbys like chicken fried with cashew nuts and *tom yam* soup with prawns.

✉ Asia Lopburi Hotel, corners of Sorasak and Phra Yam Jamkut roads ☎ (036) 411892 🕐 Lunch, dinner

Pattaya

Lobster Pot (£££)

On a pier over Pattaya Bay, this fine restaurant serves the best seafood in town. Good ambience and an extensive menu, including a superb lobster thermidor.

✉ 288 Beach Road ☎ (038) 426083 🕐 Lunch, dinner

Pan Pan San Dominico (£££)

Italian food of the highest order, serving possibly the best veal in Thailand. From the menu to the décor everything at Pan Pan is first-rate.

✉ Thanon Theprasit ☎ (038) 251874 🕐 Lunch, dinner

PIC Kitchen (££)

Fine Thai cuisine served in traditional style at low wooden tables in elegant teak houses. There is a separate air-conditioned section. Recommended.

✉ Soi 5, Pattaya Beach Road ☎ (038) 428387 🕐 Lunch, dinner

Ruen Thai (££)

A series of wooden pavilions is the setting for classical Thai dancing and high-quality Thai food. The restaurant has children's facilities including a playground.

✉ 485/3 Pattaya 2nd Road ☎ (038) 425911 🕐 Lunch, dinner

Dining Thai-style

Thai restaurants generally serve all the main dishes simultaneously rather than in a series of courses. Rice almost always plays a central role and is served in a large container. Diners are served with an individual portion of rice and then help themselves to small but frequently replenished portions of curry, soup, fish, poultry and various meat dishes, which are presented with the rice.

Southern Thailand

Dining Implements

Thais always eat rice and accompanying dishes using a fork and spoon. Knives are only used for European-style meals, as Thai food is served already cut into bite-sized pieces. Chopsticks are reserved for noodle dishes that are perceived as being Chinese in origin. (Other noodle dishes, such as *khanm jeen,* of Mon origin, are eaten with a fork and spoon.)

Cha-am

Sorndaeng (££)

Seafood cooked to perfection using Thai and European recipes. Not cheap but remarkable quality.

⊠ **Methavalai Hotel, 220 Thanon Ruamchit** ☎ **(032) 471 145-6** ◑ **Lunch, dinner**

Hat Yai

Hua Lee (££)

Popular with the local Chinese for its superb shark's fin and bird's nest soups. Open until very late.

⊠ **Thanon Niphat Uthit 3** ☎ **No telephone** ◑ **Lunch, dinner**

Hua Hin

Railway Restaurant (£££)

Decorated in the style of Hua Hin Railway Station in the 1920s. Thai, French, Italian and Chinese buffets.

⊠ **Hotel Sofitel, 1 Thanon Damnoen Kasem** ☎ **(032) 512021** ◑ **Lunch, dinner**

Rim Nam (££)

Live classical Thai music accompanies excellent Thai food served in a traditional antique Thai-style setting. The *kaeng khiaw wan* (green curry) is excellent.

⊠ **43/1 Petchkasem Beach Road** ☎ **(032) 520250** ◑ **Lunch, dinner**

Saeng Thai (££)

The oldest restaurant in Hua Hin. Reliable seafood coupled with good service. Open-air on the seafront.

⊠ **Thanon Naresdamri (near the pier)** ☎ **(032) 512144** ◑ **Lunch, dinner**

Ko Samui

Captain's Choice (£££)

One of Ko Samui's best restaurants. A good place to enjoy shark delicacies and other popular seafood like prawns, crab, squid, lobster and crayfish.

⊠ **Choeng Mon Beach** ☎ **(077) 425041** ◑ **Lunch, dinner**

Happy Elephant (£)

Good Thai dishes like grilled prawns and sweet tamarind sauce with prawn cakes grilled on fresh sugar cane sticks. Excellent seafood.

⊠ **19/1 Moo 1 Bophut** ☎ **(077) 245347** ◑ **Lunch, dinner**

Laguna Terrace (££)

Seaside restaurant offering Thai and continental cuisine. Classical Thai dancing in the evenings. Large, reasonably priced lunchtime buffet.

⊠ **Blue Lagoon Hotel, 99 Moo 2, Chaweng Beach** ☎ **(077) 422037** ◑ **Lunch, dinner**

Pakarang (££)

Dine indoors surrounded by paintings of Ko Samui, or outside under a bougainvillea trellis. The chef makes no attempt to reduce the Thai flavours unless requested.

⊠ **9 Moo 2 Tambon Bophut** ☎ **(077) 422223** ◑ **Lunch, dinner**

Krabi

Ko Tung (££)

Serves central and southern Thai seafood dishes including a first-class *tom yam thalay* (spicy seafood soup). Ko Tung is clean, friendly and reasonably priced.

⊠ **36 Thanon Kongkaa** ☎ **(075) 611522** ◑ **Lunch, dinner**

Nakhon Si Thammarat

Khrua Nakhon (£)

Enjoy authentic southern

Thai dishes in an open-style restaurant. Special dishes include *kao yum* (Southern Thai salad) and *kanom jeen* (Chinese noodles).

✉ **Bovorn Bazaar, Thanon Ratchadamnoen** ☎ **(075) 317197** ◉ **Breakfast, lunch**

Phuket
Bluefin Tavern (££)
Slightly away from Kata Beach, this pub serves Tex-Mex dishes like Texas chilli and fish chowder, Cuban black bean soup, pastrami and roast beef sandwiches.

✉ **111/17 Thanon Taina, Kata Beach** ☎ **(076) 330856** ◉ **Lunch, dinner**

Giorgio's (££)
Italian food and a comprehensive wine list served in a tropical garden. The seafood soup is recommended, as are the pasta and Swiss pastries.

✉ **Beach Road, Patong** ☎ **(076) 341193** ◉ **Lunch, dinner**

Kan Eng Seafood (££)
Superb fresh Thai seafood; the curried seafood mousse is a must. Diners make their own selection from the seafood on display. Views over Chalong Bay yacht harbour.

✉ **Chalong Bay** ☎ **(076) 381323** ◉ **Lunch, dinner**

Kiko (£££)
Fine Japanese restaurant next to the beach with ingredients freshly imported from Japan. Special dishes include sushi and sashimi.

✉ **Diamond Cliff Resort, 284 Thanon Prabarimi, Kalim Beach** ☎ **(076) 340501** ◉ **Lunch, dinner**

Lai Mai (££)
Seafood, fondue, pizza and other Thai and western dishes, near Patong Beach. Live music every night.

✉ **68 Thanon Taveewong,** ☎ **(076) 292 276–8** ◉ **Breakfast, lunch, dinner**

Metropole Café (££)
Comfortable à la carte dining in a smart setting. Choose from imported beef steak, South Chinese cuisine or fresh seafood prepared in southern Thai style.

✉ **Metropole Hotel, 1 Soi Surin, Montri Road, Phuket Town** ☎ **(076) 215050** ◉ **Dinner**

Pae Thip (££)
One of the Pearl Village Resort's three classy restaurants, set in the middle of a lake. Beautifully prepared Thai food, plus Japanese and Korean dishes. Try the Korean barbecue, cooked at the table.

✉ **Pearl Village Resort, Nai Yang Beach** ☎ **(076) 327006** ◉ **Lunch, dinner. Closed Wed**

Regatta Bar and Grill (£££)
Superb *nouvelle* cuisine from the resident European chef. One of Phuket's best restaurants, overlooking Nai Harn Bay. Live music.

✉ **Phuket Yacht Club, Nai Harn Beach** ☎ **(076) 381156** ◉ **Lunch, dinner**

Ranong
Palm Court (££)
The best restaurant in town, part of the Jansom Thara Ranong Hotel. Dim sum and Chinese noodle dishes plus Thai food like *kaeng matsaman* (Muslim curry).

✉ **2/10 Thanon Phetkasem** ☎ **(077) 811510** ◉ **Lunch, dinner**

Dining Etiquette
As in the West, it is polite to offer dishes to guests, older people and women first. It is also good manners to offer especially dainty titbits to other diners. Thais are generally fastidiously clean and admire good manners. If you adhere to this, you will be considered a *pu-di angkrit* or 'English gentleman' (or lady).

Northern Thailand

Khantoke
Traditionally northern Thai dinners are served at a *khantoke*, a low circular table usually made of rattan. Dishes include northern specialities such as *nam phrik ong*, a pork and chilli dip; *kaeng hang lay*, pork cooked with ginger; and *kep mu* or crispy pork rinds. Served with fresh vegetables and sticky rice, it is delicious.

Chiang Mai
Antique House (££)
Superb northern Thai cooking by the side of the Ping River, served amid antique Lanna furniture and handicrafts. Good central Thai food is also available. The restaurant has an early 20th-century feel.
- 71 Thanon Charoen Prathet
- (053) 276810 ⏺ Lunch, dinner

Brasserie Restaurant (££)
Open from 2PM, serving mostly central Thai dishes, seafood and some northern Thai delicacies. Very lively later in the evening, with live music by the Ping River.
- 37 Thanon Charoen Rat
- (053) 241665
- ⏺ Lunch, dinner

Kaeng Ron Ban Suan (££)
Northern Thai dishes served in a Lanna-style garden. Beautiful location at the foot of Doi Suthep. Popular with locals.
- 149/3 Soi Chom Doi Moo 2
- (053) 213762 ⏺ Lunch, dinner

Le Coq d'Or (£££)
Originally the British consul's residence now Chiang Mai's top French restaurant. Excellent food and wine.
- 68/1Thanon Ko Klang ☎ (053) 282024 ⏺ Lunch, dinner

Old Chiang Mai Cultural Centre (££)
Set in a series of old Lanna-style houses. Traditional northern-style *khantoke* dinners in peaceful surroundings, with classical dance and music.
- 185/3 Thanon Wualai
- (053) 202993-5 ⏺ Dinner

Raan Khao Soi Islam (£)
Muslim restaurant offering the best *khao soi* (a northern noodle dish) in Thailand, plus satay, samosa and mutton biriyani. Enthusiasts from Bangkok fly up to eat here.
- Thanon Charoen Prathet Soi 1 ☎ No telephone
- ⏺ Breakfast, lunch

Riverside (££)
Good mix of Thai and European food, friendly atmosphere and great river view. Packed with young Thais and visitors. Also dine on board one of their nightly cruises.
- 9/11 Thanon Charoen Rat
- (053) 243239 ⏺ Lunch, dinner

Chiang Rai
Golden Triangle International Café (££)
A reasonable selection of Thai and Western food, with some northern dishes as well. Air-conditioned, with Lanna-style décor.
- 590 Thanon Phaholyotn
- (053) 711399 ⏺ Breakfast, lunch, dinner

Yoongthong (££)
Trendy establishment serving a wide range of Thai, Chinese (both recommended) and Western dishes (rather ordinary).
- Wangcome Hotel, 869/90 Thanon Pemavibhata ☎ (053) 711800 ⏺ Lunch, dinner

Doi Mae Salong
Mae Salong Resort (££)
Yunnanese Chinese dishes in the best restaurant in town. Spectacular views across the valley. Warm up with a fruit liqueur.
- 5 Mu 1, Santikhiri ☎ (053) 765115 ⏺ Lunch, dinner

Golden Triangle [Sop Ruak]

Border View (££)

Excellent Thai, Chinese and Western food on a beautiful terrace overlooking the Mekong River in the heart of the Golden Triangle.

✉ 222 Golden Triangle, Sop Ruak ☎ (053) 784001–5
◉ Lunch, dinner

Kamphaeng Phet

Ruan Phae Rim Ping (££)

Beautiful garden restaurant beside the Ping River. Good central Thai cuisine including *kai phat pet mamuang* (fried chicken with cashew nuts).

✉ Soi 1 Thanon Thesa 2 ☎ (055) 712767 ◉ Lunch, dinner

Lampang

Riverside Bar and Restaurant (££)

Excellent Thai food on the banks of the Yom River. Live Thai folk music most nights.

✉ 328 Thanon Tipchang ☎ (054) 221861 ◉ Lunch, dinner

Mae Hong Son

Bai Fern (££)

Mostly Thai food with some simple Western dishes. One of the best places in town.

✉ Thanon Khunlum Praphat ☎ (053) 611374 ◉ Lunch, dinner

Golden Teak Restaurant (££)

Part of the Imperial Tara complex. Good Western food.

✉ 149 Moo 8, Tambon Pang Moo ☎ (053) 611021–5
◉ Breakfast, lunch, dinner

Mae Sai

Rabieng Kaew (££)

Pleasant garden restaurant serving good central and northern Thai food and regional dishes such as Korean barbecued beef.

✉ 356/2 Moo 1 Thanon Paholyothin ☎ (053) 731172/3
◉ Lunch, dinner

Nan

Da Dario (££)

Extensive range of well-prepared, authentic Italian dishes. Friendly staff and atmosphere.

✉ 37/4 Thanon Rajamnuay, Ban Prakerd ☎ (054) 750258
◉ Lunch, dinner

Siam Pochana (£)

An old wooden building housing the most reliable restaurant in Nan. Menu is all Thai and Chinese. Try the *jok* rice porridge for breakfast.

✉ Thanon Sumon Dheveraj
☎ No telephone
◉ Breakfast, lunch, dinner

Phitsanulok

Rim Nan (££)

A floating restaurant moored by the west bank of the Nan River. Pleasant ambience and cool breezes in the hot season. The house special is *neua yang* (barbecued beef) 'Genghis Khan'.

✉ 63/2 Thanon Wang Chan ☎ (055) 251446 ◉ Lunch, dinner

Sukhothai

Dream Café and Antique House (££)

Decorated with 19th- and early 20th-century Thai antiques, this place has character. Thai, Chinese and Western dishes are served here, plus many herbal liqueurs.

✉ 86/1 Thanon Singhawat
☎ (055) 612081
◉ Lunch, dinner

Khao Soi

A characteristically northern dish is *khao soi*, believed to have originated in nearby Myanmar (Burma). Chopped beef or chicken is served in a curry broth with flat wheat noodles, deep fried crispy noodles, chopped red onions, pickled cabbage and fresh lime. Add chilli to taste.

Isaan

Sticky Rice

Most Westerners, like central Thais, are well acquainted with long-grain jasmine rice *(khao suay* in Thai). In the north and especially in the northeast of Thailand, however, people prefer *khao niaw* or sticky rice. Steamed and served in a lidded wicker basket, *khao niaw* is eaten with the fingers. Locals roll the rice into a ball, dip it in an appropriate sauce and then pop it neatly into their mouths.

Chiang Khan
Mekong Riverside (£)
A beautiful setting with views over the river to Laos. Fish specials, as well as many other dishes. A good place for a cool drink at sunset.

✉ Soi 10 Thanon Chai Khong ☎ No telephone ◉ Lunch, dinner

Khon Kaen
Khrua Weh (££)
Genuine Vietnamese food plus excellent Thai and Isaan dishes served in an attractive old teak house. Try the spicy chicken and mint salad.

✉ 1/1 Thanon Klang Meuang ☎ No telephone ◉ Lunch, dinner

Parrot Restaurant (£)
Offers an extensive menu including pizza, hamburgers and a good selection of Thai dishes. Good service.

✉ Thanon Sri Chan ☎ (043) 244692 ◉ Breakfast, lunch, dinner

Loei
Sawita Bakery (£)
Basically a coffee shop that happens to serve good central Thai food and Western fast food like burgers and spaghetti. Has a fine range of cakes.

✉ 139 Thanon Charoenrat ☎ No telephone ◉ Breakfast, lunch, dinner

Mukdahan
Riverside (££)
Situated on the Mekong, this shady terrace offers mainly Thai and Chinese dishes. A good place to sit in the late afternoon with a cold beer.

✉ Thanon Samran Chai Khong ☎ (042) 612846 ◉ Lunch, dinner

Nakhon Phanom
Golden Giant Catfish (£)
Riverside restaurant specialising in the giant Mekong catfish (which can weigh up to 200kg).

✉ Thanon Sunthon Vichit ☎ (042) 511218 ◉ Lunch, dinner

Nakhon Ratchasima
Bankaew (££)
Luxurious establishment specialising in seafood but with many other dishes.

✉ 105/17–19 Thanon Jomsurangyat ☎ (044) 246512 ◉ Lunch, dinner

Krungthep Seafood (££)
Fresh seafood from the Gulf of Siam. Excellent giant prawns.

✉ Thanon Phoklang ☎ (044) 256183 ◉ Dinner

VFW Café (£)
Founded by ex-US service-men who stayed on after the Vietnam War. Serves steaks, sausages and pizzas.

✉ 167-8 Thanon Phoklang ☎ (044) 242831 ◉ Breakfast, lunch, dinner

Nong Khai
Banya Pochana (££)
Serves Thai, Chinese and Lao food and specialises in fish dishes. Beautiful views across the Mekong to the Mittraphap Bridge and Laos.

✉ 295 Thanon Rim Khong ☎ No telephone ◉ Lunch, dinner

Phanom Rung [Buriram]
Phanom Rung Historical Park (£)
The only place to eat at Phanom Rung. A series of stalls and small restaurants offering Isaan food like

papaya salad, grilled chicken, curries and sticky rice.

📧 **Phanom Rung Hill** ☎ **No telephone** 🕐 **Breakfast, lunch**

Phimai
Baitoey (£)
Good Thai and Western fare in a pleasant rustic setting. Menu includes vegetarian dishes, ice-cream and various sticky rice and coconut sweets.

📧 **Thanon Jomsudah Sadet** ☎ **(044) 471725** 🕐 **Breakfast, lunch, dinner**

Surin
Wang Petch (££)
Wide range of Thai, Chinese and Western dishes. Surin's most trendy restaurant, geared to businesspeople. Live music nightly.

📧 **104 Thanon Jitbumrung** ☎ **(044) 511274** 🕐 **Lunch, dinner**

That Phanom
Somkhane (£)
Near the triumphal arch in the central area, this small restaurant offers great Thai and Chinese fish dishes.

📧 **Thanon Kuson Ratchadamnoen** 🕐 **Breakfast, lunch, dinner**

Ubon Ratchathani
Chiokee (£)
The place to visit for a good breakfast, be it Western-style or Thai-style. A special is congee (jok), a thick porridge served with an egg and minced pork.

📧 **Thanon Kheuan Thani** 🕐 **Breakfast, lunch**

Indochine (££)
One of the best Vietnamese restaurants in Thailand. Cooking and atmosphere in an old teak house attracts diners from as far as Bangkok and Chiang Mai. Try the cha gio (spring rolls), nem nuong (spicy pork meatballs) and pho (beef noodle soup).

📧 **Wat Jaeng, Thanon Samphasit** ☎ **(045) 245584** 🕐 **Lunch, early evening**

Sincere Restaurant (££)
Tastefully decorated establishment serving fine French and Thai food. Owner and chef Khun Panee ran a French restaurant in Pattaya before retiring to Ubon.

📧 **126/1 Thanon Sappasit** ☎ **(045) 245061** 🕐 **Lunch, dinner**

Udon Thani
Ban Isaan (£)
Serves all the northeast's best-known dishes. First-rate spicy minced chicken and mint leaves (laap kai) and green papaya salad (som tam).

📧 **177–179 Thanon Adunyadet** ☎ **No telephone** 🕐 **Lunch, dinner**

Rung Thong (£)
One of the oldest restaurants in Isaan, known for its excellent curries. Also serves central and north-eastern dishes.

📧 **Thanon Prajak Silpakorn, west of the Clock Tower** ☎ **No telephone** 🕐 **Lunch, dinner**

Udom Rot (£)
Overlooks the ferry crossing point to Laos. Dishes include Vietnamese-style spring rolls, Isaan minced meats (laap) and very good fresh-water fish dishes.

📧 **193 Thanon Rim Khong** ☎ **(042) 421084** 🕐 **Breakfast, lunch, dinner**

Papaya Salad

Som tam or chopped papaya salad, is popular throughout Thailand but particularly so in the northeast. Thais prefer this delicious blend of fresh papaya, lime juice, garlic, tomatoes, ground peanuts and field crab (optional) spicy hot. A word to the wise – ask for food *mai phet* or 'not spicy' unless you are a real chilli lover.

Central Thailand

Prices

Prices are per room, per night, excluding breakfast:

£ = under 1,000 baht
££ = 1,000–2,500 baht
£££ = over 2,500 baht

Thailand is blessed with an enormous range of accommodation, from luxury island resorts to cheap-and-cheerful guest houses.

Bangkok

Asia (££)

Conveniently located for Siam Square and the World Trade Centre. Close to the banks of Saen Saep Canal, making travel to Sukhumvit by boat an easy option.

✉ **296 Thanon Phayathai**
☎ **(02) 215 0808; fax: (02) 215 4360** 🚇 **N1 Ratchathewi Station**
🚌 **79**

Dusit Thani (£££)

In the heart of Bangkok's Silom Road business district. Incredibly sumptuous, with eight restaurants and six bars. Stunning views from the rooftop Tiara Restaurant.

✉ **Thanon Rama IV** ☎ **(02) 236 0450–9; fax: (02) 236 6400** 🚇 **S2 Saladaeng Station** 🚌 **2, 4, 5**

Grand Hyatt Erawan (£££)

Luxurious, centrally located and perfect for the World Trade Centre and Ploenchit. Nearby is the venerable Erawan Shrine (➤ 36).

✉ **494 Thanon Ratchadamri**
☎ **(02) 254 1234; fax: (02) 254 6308** 🚇 **E1 Chidlom Station**
🚌 **4, 5**

Mandarin Bangkok (££)

Fresh, airy rooms and all the facilities associated with a luxury hotel. Reasonable room rates for the quality.

✉ **662 Thanon Rama IV** ☎ **(02) 238 0230; fax: (02) 237 1620**
🚌 **1, 7**

Oriental (£££)

Long Bangkok's top hotel, it has acquired many rivals in terms of luxury – but not character (➤ 37).

✉ **48 Soi Oriental**
☎ **(02) 659 9000; fax: (02) 659 0000** 🚇 **S6 Saphan Taksin Station** 🚌 **2, 4**

Regent (£££)

Luxury hotel offering every conceivable amenity from ballroom dancing to yoga. Centrally located facing the Royal Bangkok Sports Club.

✉ **155 Thanon Ratchadamri**
☎ **(02) 251 6127; fax: (02) 253 9195** 🚇 **S1 Ratchadamri Station** 🚌 **4, 5**

Rembrandt (££)

Luxury facilities including six restaurants; Mexican and Indian cuisine are featured. Five minutes by car from Queen Sirikit Convention Centre – on a good day.

✉ **Soi 18 Thanon Sukhumvit**
☎ **(02) 261 7100; fax: (02) 261 7017** 🚇 **E4 Asoke Station**
🚌 **1, 8, 11, 38**

Royal (£)

One of Bangkok's oldest and most venerable hotels, close to the Grand Palace. In 1992 the lobby was the scene of some of the worst excesses against pro-democracy demonstrators by the army.

✉ **2 Thanon Ratchadamnoen Klang** ☎ **(02) 222 9111; fax: (02) 224 2083** 🚌 **7, 9, 11**

Shangri-La (£££)

One of Bangkok's best hotels; even offers helicopter transfer service to the airport. Serves high tea.

✉ **89 Soi Wat Suan Phlu**
☎ **(02) 236 7777; fax: (02) 236 8579** 🚇 **S6 Saphan Thaksin Station** 🚌 **2, 4, 5**

White Lodge (£)

A small, friendly place; good value for money. Close to Siam Square, Mahboonkrong Shopping Centre and Jim Thompson's house.

✉ **36/8 Soi Kasem San 1** ☎ **(02) 216 8867; fax: (02) 216 8228**
🚇 **Center Siam Station** 🚌 **1, 8**

Ayuthaya

Ayuthaya Grand (£)
Comfortable hotel slightly away from the main part of town. Nightclub, coffee shop and pool.
✉ 55/5 Thanon Rotchana
☎ (035) 335483; fax: (035) 335492

Ayuthaya Riverside (££)
Probably the best hotel in Ayuthaya, with good views of the river and town. Excellent Chinese restaurant, bowling alley and snooker club.
✉ 27/2 Thanon Rotchana ☎ (035) 243139; fax: (035) 244139

U-Thong Inn (£)
Well positioned for all the main historical sights. Facilities include a pool and a sauna room. New wing is better value than the old.
✉ 210 Thanon Rotchana
☎ (035) 242236–9; fax: (035) 242235

Kanchanaburi

Felix Kanchanaburi Swissotel River Kwai (£££)
Luxurious resort beside the River Kwai. Beautifully landscaped gardens plus tennis courts and large swimming pools.
✉ 9/1 Moo 3 Thamakhan
☎ (034) 515061; fax: (034) 515095

Kasem Island Resort (£)
Thatched cottages and houseboats to the south of the town on a small island. Offers rafting, fishing and a pleasant bar.
✉ Kasem Island, near Thanon Chukkadon ☎ (034) 513359

River Kwai Hotel (££)
An old favourite away from the river in the town. Well-appointed rooms, disco, coffee shop and pool.
✉ 284/3-16 Thanon Saengchuto
☎ (034) 513348; fax: (034) 511269

Ko Samet

Samet Ville Resort (££)
Private and chic, well away from the sprawl of bungalows on other more developed beaches. Fan and air-conditioned bungalows.
✉ Wai Bay ☎ (038) 652561; fax: (02) 246 3196

Vongdeuan Resort (£)
One of the better resorts on the island. Comfortable air-conditioned bungalows with running water in beautiful (but noisy) Wong Deuan Bay.
✉ Wong Deuan Bay ☎ (038) 651777; fax: (038) 651819

Lopburi

Lopburi Inn Resort (££)
Situated out of town to the west, Lopburi's newest and best hotel. Excellent facilities including sauna, fitness centre and large pool.
✉ 144 Tambon Tha Sala
☎ (036) 420777; fax: (036) 412010

Pattaya

Grand Jomtien Palace (££)
In the middle of Jomtien Beach some way from Pattaya's raunchy nightlife.
✉ 356 Jomtien Beach Road
☎ (038) 231405–8; fax: (038) 231404

Royal Cliff Beach Hotel (£££)
Overlooking South Pattaya and Jomtien Bay, this is one of Pattaya's oldest and best hotels. Sports facilities and eight excellent restaurants.
✉ 378 Thanon Pratamnak ☎ (038) 250421–3; fax: (038) 250511

Toilets
Western-style toilets and bathroom facilities are increasingly the norm, but up-country and at smaller or older hotels you may encounter squat toilets with water and a jug rather than toilet paper. Either carry your own paper or learn from the locals and use your right hand to pour and your left to wash with! Many modern toilets have a spray to wash with, as well as toilet paper.

Southern Thailand

Mosquitoes

Malaria is a problem near the borders with Myanmar (Burma), Cambodia and Laos, in hilly, forested areas and on certain islands, notably Ko Chang. In big cities you should be safe, although some hotels still offer mosquito nets and it is wise to use a mosquito repellent as a precaution.

It is best to ask your GP for the latest advice about whether to take anti-malarial tablets during your visit.

Hua Hin

Sofitel Central (£££)

A fine old colonial-style hotel by the beach, with a topiary garden. This is the place filmed as the French Embassy in Phnom Penh in the film *The Killing Fields*.

✉ 1 Thanon Damnoen Kasem ☎ (032) 512021–35; fax: (032) 511014

Ko Samui

Central Samui Beach Resort (£££)

In a beautiful garden setting, towards the middle of Chaweng Beach, offering a health centre and tennis courts. Just 15 minutes' drive from the airport.

✉ 38/2 Moo 3 Borpud, Chaweng Beach ☎ (077) 230500; fax: (077) 422385

Coral Cove Chalet (££)

Beautifully located resort set in a cove framed by coconut palms. Good swimming pool and excellent restaurant.

✉ 210 Coral Cove Beach, Lamai ☎ (077) 422173; fax: (077) 422496

Imperial Boat House (£££)

A unique resort with beautifully decorated old teak rice barges for accommodation and a boat-shaped pool. Extensive facilities.

✉ 83 Moo 5 Tambon Bophut ☎ (077) 425041–52; fax: (077) 425460-1

Krabi

Krabi Resort (££)

Stay in a luxury bungalow and watch the sun set over the outlying islands in the Andaman Sea, then party at the resort's videotheque.

✉ Moo 2 Tambon Ao Nang ☎ (075) 637031; fax: (075) 637052

Phuket

Amanpuri Resort (£££)

Perhaps Phuket's most exclusive resort. Isolated and tranquil, it attracts the cream of Thai society. Yachts are available for cruising.

✉ Pansea Beach ☎ (076) 324333; fax: (076) 324100

Dusit Laguna Resort (£££)

Between a beautiful lagoon and the sea. A large resort with superb restaurants and health facilities.

✉ 390 Thanon Sri Sunthorn, Cherngtalay ☎ (076) 324320–32; fax: (076) 324174

Diamond Cliff Resort (£££)

At the northern end of Patong Beach, set in extensive grounds overlooking Patong Bay. Two good restaurants.

✉ 284 Thanon Prabarimi, Patong ☎ (076) 340501–6; fax: (076) 340507

Felix Karon Phuket (£££)

At the northern end of Karon Beach. Good children's facilities. Great Southern Thai restaurant.

✉ 4/8 Thanon Patak, Karon Beach ☎ (076) 396666–75; fax: (076) 396853

Marina Cottage (££)

Surrounded by coconut palms at the southern end of Karon Beach.

✉ 119 Mu 4 Thanon Patak, Karon Beach ☎ (076) 330625; fax: (076) 330516

Songkhla

Samila Beach (££)

Located on Samila Beach, next to the Songkhla golf course.

✉ 8 Thanon Ratchadamnoen ☎ (074) 440222; fax: (074) 440442

Northern Thailand

Chiang Mai

Amari Rincome (££)
Renowned for its reasonably priced lunch buffets and for promoting a wide range of international cuisines through regular food fairs. A good place for children.

✉ 1 Nimmanhaemin Road.
☎ (053) 221123; fax: (053) 221915

Chatree Guest House (£)
A short walk from the many silversmith shops on nearby Wua Lai Road. A friendly, relaxed atmosphere with a small but pleasant pool area.

✉ 11/10 Thanon Suriyawong
☎ (053) 279221; fax: (053) 279085

Chiang Inn (££)
As close to Chiang Mai's fabled night bazaar as it is possible to be. Also features a popular disco, The Wall, and a fine restaurant.

✉ 100 Thanon Chang Klan ☎ (053) 270070–6; fax: (053) 274299

Chiang Mai Plaza (££)
Next to Chiang Mai's busy night bazaar area, close to the river. Live music in the coffee bar, often featuring popular Filipino musicians.

✉ 92 Thanon Si Donchai ☎ (053) 270036–50; fax: (053) 279459

Diamond Riverside (£)
On the banks of the Ping River, a short walk from the night bazaar. Within the hotel grounds an old teak house serves as a restaurant.

✉ 33/10 Thanon Charoen Prathet ☎ (053) 270080–5; fax: (053) 279483

Lai Thai Guest House (£)
Good value, basic accommo-dation, with a pool, by the moat surrounding Chiang Mai's old city. A perfect location if you happen to be in Chiang Mai during April's water-throwing festival.

✉ 111/4–5 Thanon Kotchasan
☎ (053) 271725; fax: (053) 272724

Orchid (££)
The top hotel in the past, popular with visiting royalty. Standards are still high. Fine restaurants and wine cellar.

✉ 23 Thanon Huai Gaew
☎ (053) 222099; fax: (053) 221625

Regent Chiang Mai (£££)
In the Mae Sa Valley surrounded by 8 hectares of landscaped gardens with lakes, rice fields and water buffaloes.

✉ Mae Rim–Samoeng Old Road, Chiang Mai ☎ (053) 298190; fax: (053) 298190

River View Lodge (£)
In the heart of Chiang Mai, overlooking the Ping River. Large, almost Swiss-style chalet with rooms containing traditional Lanna furnishings. Amenities include a pool.

✉ 25 Thanon Charoen Prathet Soi 2 ☎ (053) 271110; fax: (053) 279019

Royal Princess (££)
In the commercial heart of Chiang Mai. Popular with businesspeople, especially because of its Japanese and Chinese restaurants.

✉ 112 Thanon Chang Klan ☎ (053) 281033; fax: (053) 281044.

Westin Chiang Mai (£££)
Chiang Mai's top hotel offering fine views of the Ping River with the most expensive and exclusive rooms in town. Recent visiting dignitaries include the President of China.

✉ 318/1 Chiang Mai–Lamphun Road ☎ (053) 275300; fax: (053) 275299

Laundry
Almost every hotel and guest house offers an efficient, clean and cheap laundry service. Clothing is normally returned washed, dried and ironed within 24 hours, although a faster service is usually available on request.

Northern Thailand

Tax and Tipping
Better (or more expensive) hotels generally charge a 10 per cent service charge and 7.5 per cent government tax. Guest houses and more reasonably priced hotels do not charge any tax, nor is tipping required. The same is true in restaurants. Increasingly, however, a small tip is expected, and like anywhere else in the world is much appreciated.

Chiang Rai
Dusit Island Resort (££)
Large, luxurious hotel set on its own island in the middle of the Kok River. Plenty of local boat traffic makes for an interesting afternoon watching the passing parade.
⊠ 1129 Thanon Kraisorasit ☎ (053) 715777; fax: (053) 715801

Golden Triangle Inn (£)
Attractive landscaped grounds include a Japanese-Thai garden. Room rates cover an American breakfast. Also runs a helpful travel agency and car rental service.
✚ 590 Thanon Phahonyothin ☎ (053) 716996; fax: (053) 713963

Wangcome Hotel (££)
In the heart of Chiang Rai. Comfortable rooms, coffee shop, disco and swimming pool.
⊠ 869/90 Thanon Premawiphat ☎ (053) 711800; fax: (053) 712973

Golden Triangle [Sop Ruak]
Le Meridien Baan Boran (£££)
Fabulous luxury resort using a mix of classic northern Thai forms and contemporary hotel design. Mountain biking, elephant rides, excursions and boat trips.
⊠ 229 Moo 1 Golden Triangle, Sop Ruak ☎ (053) 784084; fax: (053) 784090

Lampang
Lampang Wiengthong Hotel (£)
A plush hotel in downtown Lampang, offering all the modern conveniences you would expect from a much more expensive place.
⊠ 138/109 Thanon Phahonyothin ☎ (054) 225801; fax: (054) 225803

Mae Hong Son
Imperial Tara (££)
A beautifully situated resort slightly to the south of the main town. Rooms are set amid tropical gardens and there is a good restaurant.
⊠ 149 Moo 8, Tambon Pang Moo ☎ (053) 611272; fax: (053) 611252

Nan
Dheveraj Hotel (£)
The only reasonable hotel in Nan, but still fairly basic. Large well-kept rooms.
⊠ 466 Thanon Sumonthewarat ☎ (054) 710078; fax: (054) 771365

Phitsanulok
Sappraiwan Grand Hotel and Resort (££)
First-class resort with rooms ranging from singles to three-bedroom chalets. Set amid mountains on 120 hectares of landscaped grounds. Club house, fitness centre, paddle boats and more.
⊠ 79 Moo 2, Tambon Kaengsopha, Amphur Wangthong ☎ (055) 293293; fax: (055) 293339

Rajapruk Hotel (£)
A typical middle-to-upper-range Thai provincial hotel – clean, comfortable, with modern facilities including satellite television in all rooms and a pool.
⊠ 99/9 Thanon Phra Ong Dam ☎ (055) 258477; fax: (055) 212737

Sukhothai
Sawaddiphong (£)
A clean and comfortable old hotel in New Sukhothai. Top restaurant specialising in Thai-style *suki-yaki* and fine Thai and Chinese dishes.
⊠ 56/2-5 Thanon Singhawat ☎ (055) 611567; fax: (055) 612268

Isaan

Buriram [Phanom Rung]

Sang Rung Interpark (£)

The best hotel in Buriram, and the nearest good accommodation to Phanom Rung Khmer temple.

✉ Buriram–Huai Ra Road
☎ (044) 614483; fax: (044) 612414

Khon Kaen

Sofitel Raja Orchid (£££)

The northeast's most luxurious hotel with restaurants serving Thai, Italian and Vietnamese food. Large underground entertainment complex and disco.

✉ 9/9 Thanon Prachasamran
☎ (043) 322155; fax: (043) 322150

Loei

Thai Udom (£)

Adequate facilities in a typical up-country Thai hotel. Probably better than anywhere else in Loei, and a good base to explore nearby Phu Kradung National Park.

✉ Thanon Charoenrat ☎ (042) 811763; fax: (042) 830187

Mukdahan

Mukdahan Grand (££)

The best accommodation in Mukdahan. Offers tours to the Lao city of Savannakhet.

✉ 78 Thanon Songnang Sathit
☎ (042) 612020; fax: (042) 612021

Nakhon Ratchasima (Khorat)

Royal Princess Khorat (££)

Decorated in northeastern Thai style, this first-class hotel has a large pool, business centre and the famed Empress Chinese restaurant.

✉ 1137 Thanon Suranari ☎ (044) 256629–35; fax: (044) 256601

Sima Thani (££)

Nakhon Ratchasima's top hotel is some distance from the middle of town. All rooms have satellite television, and are clean and spacious. The large atrium is decorated with various Khmer-style sculptures.

✉ Thanon Mittraphap ☎ (044) 213100; fax: (044) 213121

Nong Khai Mekong Royal

Nong Khai (££)

Close to the Friendship Bridge spanning the Mekong between Thailand and Laos, this luxury hotel offers the best accommodation in town. Pool and coffee shop.

✉ 222 Thanon Had Jommani
☎ (042) 420024; fax: (042) 421280

Surin

Thong Tarin (£)

Surin's best hotel with economic room rates that include a buffet breakfast. Large massage parlour.

✉ 60 Thanon Sirirat ☎ (044) 514281–8; fax: (045) 511580

Ubon Ratchathani

Regent Palace (££)

Large, comfortable, provincial hotel with cocktail lounge, coffee shop, in-room satellite television and snooker hall.

✉ 265-271 Thanon Chayangkun
☎ (045) 245046–7; fax: (045) 255489

Udon Thani

Charoen (££)

Large hotel, with a budget old wing and a more expensive new wing. Great facilities including disco, cocktail lounge and pool.

✉ 549 Thanon Phosri ☎ (042) 248155; fax: (042) 241093

Booking Ahead

Booking accommodation in advance is easy, whether at the airport, major railway and bus stations, or through the ubiquitous and helpful travel agents. Similarly air, train and bus tickets are all bookable in advance.

Handicrafts, Antiques & Markets

Counterfeits and Fakes

Thailand was once known as the place to go for counterfeit Gucci, Louis Vuitton products, not to mention imitation Nike, Benetton and a wide range of other designer goods. This is increasingly not the case as the Thai authorities are cracking down on fake goods. But beware – a wide range of computer software is still available at many outlets.

Bangkok

Chatuchak Market (➤ 16)

This sprawling market, also known as the Weekend Market, sells everything from Buddha images and ceramics to musical instruments, plus a vast range of clothing. On an average weekend, about 200,000 people visit daily.

🖂 **Southern end of Chatuchak Park, off Thanon Phahonyothin** 🕙 **Sat–Sun 8–6** 🚇 **N8 Mor Chit Station** 🚌 **2, 3, 9, 10, 13**

Gaysorn Plaza

Shops within the plaza sell a variety of household accessories in contemporary and antique Thai style.

🖂 **Next to Le Meridien Hotel, Thanon Ploenchit** 🚇 **E1 Chidlom Station** 🚌 **4, 5, 11, 13**

Pratunam Market

A large market complex hidden away from the main roads surrounding it. Specialises in newly designed clothing at exceptionally cheap prices.

🖂 **Junction of Thanon Phetburi and Thanon Ratchaprarop** 🚌 **4, 5, 11, 12, 13**

Chiang Mai

Hang Dong and Ban Thawai

Two villages, 15km to the south of Chiang Mai, selling furniture (some of which is superb), antiques, woodcarvings and ceramics.

🖂 **Hang Dong, Route 108**

Night Bazaar

Chiang Mai's premier tourist market sells goods ranging from Akha hill-tribe headdresses to exquisite woodcarvings. Prices are excellent, but do bargain. A good place for authentic tribal objects is The Lost Heavens at stall 21.

🖂 **Thanon Chang Khlan**

Baw Sang Village

Hand-painted umbrellas and fans in a myriad of shapes, designs and sizes, produced in a small village 9km to the east of Chiang Mai.

🖂 **Baw Sang Village, Route 1006**

Chiang Rai

Chiang Rai Handicrafts Centre

Excellent place to pick up all sorts of northern Thai and hill-tribe paraphernalia, including beautiful Akha shoulder bags.

🖂 **273 Thanon Phahonyothin**

Khon Kaen

Suun Silapahattakam Pheun Baan

This handicraft centre in Chonabot sells the locally produced *mat-mii* silk, justly famous throughout Thailand and beyond.

🖂 **Thanon Pho Sii Sa-aat, Chonabot, Khon Kaen**

Nong Khai

Village Weaver Handicrafts

A fabric centre specialising in beautifully woven items, including ready-to-wear clothing. Also excellent hand-dyed cotton.

🖂 **786/1 Thanon Prajak, Nong Khai**

Phuket

The Loft Art Gallery

A variety of contemporary art can be found in the upstairs section of this tastefully renovated shophouse. The downstairs houses a selection of Asian antiques.

🖂 **36 Thanon Thalang** ☎ **(076) 258160**

Department Stores & Supermarkets

Bangkok

Future Park Rangsit
Now Southeast Asia's largest shopping complex, with more than 400 shops and five of Thailand's leading department stores. It also has many restaurants and cinemas.
✉ **Vibhavadi–Rangsit Highway, 8km north of Bangkok Inter-national Airport** 🚌 **4, 10, 29**

Mahboonkrong
A massive shopping complex near Siam Square. All manner of items are sold and prices are very reasonable. Tokyu Department Store, within the complex, has a well-stocked supermarket.
✉ **Junction of Thanon Rama I and Thanon Phayathai** 🚈 **Center Siam Station** 🚌 **1, 2, 8**

Peninsula Plaza
A trendy plaza with a good selection of shops, including a branch of Asia Books, Thailand's premier English-language book chain.
✉ **Thanon Ratchadamri** 🚈 **E1 Chidlom Station** 🚌 **4, 5**

World Trade Centre
Another huge complex with everything from high-end boutiques to the best music shops in Bangkok. It also houses the very chic Zen Department Store and an ice-skating rink.
✉ **Junction of Thanon Ratchadamri and Thanon Rama I** 🚈 **E1 Chidlom Station** 🚌 **1, 4, 5, 8**

Chiang Mai

Airport Plaza
Located near Chiang Mai International Airport with a Robinson's department store in the same building. The Tops Supermarket in the basement is one of the best in Chiang Mai.
✉ **Thanon Om Muang**

Kad Suan Kaew
This shopping complex includes a branch of Central Department Store and has a large supermarket on the basement floor.
✉ **Thanon Huay Kaew**

Mae Ping Superstore
One of the best selections of Western food, wine and beer to be found in Chiang Mai.
✉ **Thanon Chotana**

Nakhon Ratchasima

Big C
Big C shopping complexes can be found in many of the larger central and northeast towns. This one has a good supermarket and plenty of small eating places, including American fast-food outlets.
✉ **Thanon Mittaphap**

Pattaya

Mike Shopping Mall
Mainly a clothes arcade, but there is a small supermarket within the complex.
✉ **262 Moo 10, Pattaya Beach Road**

Phuket

Robinson Ocean Plaza
Clothes boutiques, fast-food restaurants and a large supermarket attached to a branch of Robinson's department store.
✉ **Ong Sim Phai Road, Phuket Town**

Antiques and Buddha Images
As in most countries, it is illegal to export valuable antiquities without a licence. That said, Thai artisans produce an amazing range of authentic-looking repro-duction antiquities that are also reasonably priced. Note that Buddha images, whether old or new, should not be exported without a licence. This is because the Thais do not wish Buddha images to be used as lampstands or for other non-religious purposes. They believe this demeans the Buddha.

Books & Magazines

English-Language Newspapers

Thailand has a remarkably free press and produces two of the finest English-language newspapers in Asia. *The Nation* and *Bangkok Post* are both quality productions, to the extent that the Thai elite and middle classes prefer them to newspapers in the vernacular. They even follow the European and North American sports scene in depth. Occasional news sheets are produced for tourists in German, French and Japanese.

Thailand's three bookshop chains, Asia Books, Bookazine and Duang Kamol (DK) Book House, are good for new books and magazines. Asia Books, with Bangkok's best selection of English-language titles on Asia, is at Bangkok and Thailand's international airports; DK Books and Bookazine are in most towns and cities.

Bangkok

Asia Books (main branch)
New English-language novels and large format coffee-table books on Asia.
✉ Soi 15, 221 Thanon Sukhumvit ☎ (02) 252 7277 🚇 E4 Asoke Station 🚌 1, 8, 11

Asia Books (Landmark Plaza)
✉ Floors 1 and 3, Sois 2 and 3 Thanon Sukhumvit ☎ (02) 252 5839 🚇 E3 Nana Station 🚌 1, 8, 11, 13, 38

Asia Books (World Trade Centre)
✉ Junction of Thanon Ratchadamri and Thanon Rama I 🚇 E1 Chidlom Station 🚌 1, 4, 5, 8

Bookazine (Siam)
Excellent selection of international magazines.
✉ 286 Siam Square, Thanon Rama I 🚇 Center Siam 🚌 1, 2, 8

Chatuchak Market (► 16)
Second-hand English magazines and novels.
✉ Southern end of Chatuchak Park, off Phahonyothin Road 🕐 Sat–Sun 8–6 🚇 N8 Mor Chit Station 🚌 2, 3, 9, 10, 13

DK Book House (main branch)
English-language novels and computer books.
✉ 244–6 Soi 2, Siam Square ☎ (02) 251 1467 🚇 Center Siam Station 🚌 1, 2, 8

DK Book House (Sukhumvit branch)
Latest fiction titles.
✉ Thanon Sukhumvit 🚇 E3 Nana Station 🚌 1, 8, 11, 13

Elite Book House
Second-hand books and periodicals.
✉ 593/5 Thanon Sukhumvit ☎ (02) 258 0221 🚇 Phromphong 🚌 2, 4, 5

Shaman Books
Second-hand novels, maps and guidebooks; new books.
✉ 71 Thanon Khao San ☎ (02) 629 0418 🚌 11, 12, 14

Teck Heng Bookstore
Books on Southeast Asia.
✉ 1326 New Road (between Oriental Avenue and Thanon Silom), Pratunam ☎ (02) 234 1836 🚇 S6 Saphan Taksin Station 🚌 2, 4, 5

Chiang Mai

DK Book House
Cultural books on Thailand, Burma and Laos.
✉ 7/1 Thanon Kotchasan ☎ (053) 206995

Lost Bookshop
Second-hand novels, biographies and art books.
✉ 34/3 Thanon Ratchamankha

Suriwong Book Centre
Stationery, guidebooks and books on Southeast Asia.
✉ 54/1-5 Thanon Si Donchai ☎ (053) 281052

Phuket

The Books
English-language magazines.
✉ 53–55 Phuket Road

Gems, Jewellery & Silk

Bangkok

Asian Institute of Gemmological Sciences
Learn the art of gemmology. The institute will also authenticate any gems you may have.

✉ **33rd Floor, Jewellery Trade Centre, 919/1 Thanon Silom** ☎ **(02) 267 4315–9** 🚌 **2, 4, 5**

Gemopolis
Free Trade Zone for all sorts of gems and jewellery shopping so tourists enjoy duty-free privileges.

✉ **Gemopolis Industrial Estate, 47/31 Moo 4 Thanon Sukhapiban 2** ☎ **(02) 727 0022;** fax: **(02) 727 0099** 🚌 **12, 44**

Jim Thompson
A superb collection of silk items including dresses, ties, cushion covers and personal and household accessories.

✉ **9 Thanon Surawong** ☎ **(02) 234 4900; fax: (02) 236 6777** 🚌 **2, 7**

Johnny's Gems
A long-established place for set jewellery.

✉ **199 Thanon Fuang Nakhon, off Thanon Charoen Krung** ☎ **(02) 224 4065** 🚌 **4**

Silk of Thailand
Producers and dealers of Thai silk, using traditional methods and natural dyes.

✉ **77/165 Rajathevee Tower, Thanon Phayathai** ☎ **(02) 653 7124** Ⓜ **Phayathai** 🚌 **2, 3**

Shinawatra Thai Silk
A fine selection of silk products and other textiles. They have another branch in Chiang Mai.

✉ **Thanon Sathorn Tai, near Soi Suan Plu** ☎ **(02) 286 9991** 🚌 **17, 22, 62**

Chiang Mai

Jolie Femme
A large showroom plus a silk factory where you can watch the complete process of silk manufacture under one roof.

✉ **8/3 Chiang Mai–San Kamphaeng Road** ☎ **(053) 247222; fax: (053) 247887**

Lanna Thai
A fine selection of traditional Chiang Mai silver jewellery and other decorative silverware.

✉ **79 Thanon San Kamphaeng** ☎ **(053) 338015; fax: (053) 338684**

Le Bombyx
Long-established silk experts, producing all sorts of products from picture frames to lampshades.

✉ **120/11 Moo 3, Chiang Mai–San Kamphaeng Road** ☎ **(053) 339022; fax: (053) 338701**

Nova Collection
Includes a gallery and a school with daily and weekly courses in jewellery production.

✉ **201 Thanon Tapae** ☎ **(053) 273058**

Shiraz Co Ltd
Reputable dealer, selling all types of gems and jewellery. Buy from stock or order to suit.

✉ **170 Thanon Tapae** ☎ **(053) 252382; fax: (053) 252381**

Phuket

Pearl Centre
Phuket is a good source of fine quality pearls. The centre has some good bargains.

✉ **83 Ranong Road, Soi Phutorn** ☎ **(076) 211707**

Jewellery Scams
Many visitors are still taken in by gem tricksters in Bangkok and elsewhere. Beware of unsolicited approaches by individuals promising special sales or the opportunity to 'buy cheap and sell dear' when you return home. Unless you really know your gems, ask yourself why the salesman would let someone else take the profit instead of selling the gems on the international market himself.

Bangkok & Central

Thais and Children
Thais love children and are very good with them. Do not be surprised if they make a great fuss over your offspring, especially if they have blonde hair and blue eyes.

Bangkok
Ancient City
Best visited with the Samut Prakan Crocodile Farm and Zoo (➤ this page). A huge park faithfully reproducing scaled-down versions of Thailand's most famous sights.
☒ Old Sukhumvit Highway, Bangpu, Samut Prakan ☎ (02) 323 9253 ⏰ Daily 8–5 🚌 7, 8, 11 (Samut Prakan terminal, then minibus 36)

Dream World Amusement Park
An amusement park on a grand scale, with lots of rides and shows, including Snowland, Uncle Tom's Farm and the Magic Cabaret Show.
☒ KM7, Rangsit–Nakhon Nayok Highway (Klong 3) ☎ (02) 533 1152; fax: (02) 533 1899 ⏰ Mon–Fri 10–5, Sat–Sun 10–7 🚌 21, 95

Dusit Zoo
In the middle of town, with a wide variety of birds, mammals and reptiles (including the rare Komodo dragon from Indonesia). A good retreat from the hustle and bustle of Bangkok.
☒ Thanon Ratchawithi, near Chitlada Palace ☎ (02) 281 2000 ⏰ Daily 9–6 🚌 3, 10

Safari World
Billed as the largest open zoo in the world, Safari World is divided into two parts – the 5km Safari Park drive featuring various land animals and the Marine Park, exhibiting marine and rare animals.
☒ 99 Ramindra 1, Minburi ☎ (02) 518 1000 ⏰ Mon–Fri 9–5:30, Sat–Sun 9–6

Samut Prakan Crocodile Farm and Zoo
The world's largest crocodile farm with more than 30,000 of the creatures. Daily crocodile wrestling plus other attractions including a dinosaur museum and a zoo.
☒ Old Sukhumvit Highway, Samut Prakan ☎ (02) 703 4891–5 ⏰ Daily 7–6 🚌 7, 8, 11 (Samut Prakan terminal, then minibus S1, S80)

Siam Park
About 10km northeast of Bangkok. Features a man-made sea with artificial surf, water slides and beautifully landscaped gardens. Also has a funfair with scary rides.
☒ 101 Mu 4 Sukhaphiban 2 Road, Minburi ☎ (02) 517 0075 ⏰ Mon–Fri 10–6, Sat–Sun 9–7

Chonburi
Si Racha Tiger Farm
The world's largest collection of tigers, with a breeding facility vital to the species' continuance.
☒ 341 Mu 3, Nongkham, Si Racha, Chonburi Province ☎ (038) 296556 ⏰ Daily 8–6

Pattaya
Elephant Village
A great family attraction, one of the few in Pattaya. The elephants put on daily shows such as log rolling and a game of football.
☒ To the east of Pattaya, off Thanon Sukhumvit ☎ (038) 249175 ⏰ Daily 9–6

Pattaya Kart Speedway
With a circuit at slightly over a kilometre long, this is a fun place to spend an afternoon. Different powered vehicles for adults and children.
☒ 248/2 Thanon Thepprasit ☎ (038) 422044 ⏰ Daily 9:30–9:30

North & South

Chiang Mai

Chiang Mai Zoo
A beautiful zoo 6km from the middle of town at the foot of the Doi Suthep mountain. You can drive a vehicle around the zoo, but if you are walking be warned that it is particularly hilly.

✉ **Thanon Huay Kaew** 🕐 **Daily 8–5**

Mae Sa Elephant Camp
Two daily shows. Rides can be taken for different lengths of time: 5–10 minutes will cost 80 baht; 30 minutes as much as 600 baht.

✉ **R1096, KM 10 (the road to Samoeng)** ☎ **(053) 297060** 🕐 **Daily shows 8 and 9:40**

Mae Sa Snake Farm
Three daily 30-minute shows in which king cobras and banded kraits are milked and made to perform acts. Many other snakes to look at.

✉ **KM 3, 60–61 Moo 6, Mae Rim** ☎ **(053) 860719** 🕐 **Daily shows 11:30, 2.15 and 3:30**

Sainumphung Orchid and Butterfly Farm
Lots of beautiful orchids to see and buy and a butterfly farm where children learn about the life of a butterfly.

✉ **60–61 Moo 1, Rim Tai, Mae Rim** ☎ **(053) 297892** 🕐 **Daily 7–5**

Phuket

Aquarium and Marine Biological Research Centre
Hundreds of tropical fish and other marine species found mostly in local waters are exhibited in this beautifully situated aquarium.

✉ **Route 4129, at the tip of Phanwa Cape (10km from Phuket Town)** ☎ **(076) 391128** 🕐 **Daily 8:30–4**

Dino Park
This is Fred Flintstone's kitchen gone mad, billed as a 'prehistoric outdoor entertainment and dining complex'! A mini golf course winds its way past dinosaurs and a volcano.

✉ **Karon Beach** ☎ **(076) 300625** 🕐 **Daily 1–11**

Fantasea
A cultural theme park, open in the evenings, spread over 56 hectares, that explores Thailand's 'Myths, Mysteries and Magic'.

✉ **99 Moo 3 Kamala Beach** ☎ **(076) 271222; fax: (076) 271333** 🕐 **Wed–Mon 5PM–11PM**

Paintball Asia Top Gun
A harmless and fun day out for the whole family; paintball games have become quite a craze in Southeast Asia.

✉ **Chalong Bay, Chalong Shooting Range Complex** ☎ **(076) 381667; fax: (076) 381655** 🕐 **Daily 9–6**

Phuket Butterfly Garden and Aquarium
Spread over 2,800sq m, the three main areas are Butterfly Garden, Marine World and Insect Room.

✉ **71/6 Moo 5 Soi Panaeng, Yaowarat Road** ☎ **(076) 215616; fax: (076) 210860** 🕐 **Daily 9–5:30**

Phuket Seashell Museum
One of the world's most valuable collections of seashells on display. Numerous rarities and freaks including the world's largest golden pearl and a shell weighing 250kg.

✉ **Rawai Beach** ☎ **(076) 381266/74** 🕐 **Daily 8–7**

Child Prices
Half prices for children up to the age of 12 apply at most important destinations such as museums and parks. If you can read Thai, however, you may discover that the rate for overseas children is still about double the rate for Thai adults. Grin and bear it – westerners are still generally thought of as being very wealthy.

Cultural Activities

Thai Culture

Ancient and sophisticated, Thai culture is based on the Indic tradition of South Asia transmitted to Southeast Asia via the religions of first Hinduism then Buddhism. The cultural intermediaries for this transfer were the early Khmer and Mon civilisations of the region. The great Hindu epic the *Ramayana* (in Thai *Ramakien)* is still omni-present in traditional dance, painting and puppetry, with the Buddhist *Jataka* (Buddha life-cycle stories) also making a major contribution. Traditional Thai art forms such as classical dancing, classical music, shadow puppetry (in the south), food sculpting and mural painting flourish with government and royal patronage.

Ayuthaya
Chao Sam Phraya National Museum

Large selection of Ayuthayan period Buddhist sculpture.

✉ **Thanon Rotchana**
🕐 **Wed– Sun 9–4**

Bangkok
Jim Thompson's House (➤ 36)

A fabulous collection of Southeast Asian art housed in a traditional Thai residence once owned by an American silk entrepreneur.

✉ **6 Soi Kasemsan 2, off Thanon Rama 1** ☎ **(02) 215 0122**
🕐 **Mon–Sat 9–5** 🚇 **Center Siam Station** 🚌 **1, 2, 8**

National Museum (➤ 37)

Southeast Asia's largest museum holds a fine collection of ceramics, textiles, woodcarvings and weaponry, plus traditional musical instruments.

✉ **Thanon Na Phra That**
☎ **(02) 215 8173** 🕐 **Wed–Sun 9–4** 🚌 **7, 9, 11, 39**

National Theatre

Traditional performances of both *khŏn* and *lákhon*. *Khŏn* is a formal masked dance drama based around the *Ramakien; lákhon* is a more general form of dance.

✉ **Thanon Chao Fa, near Phra Pin Klao Bridge** ☎ **(02) 224 1342** 🕐 **7 performances monthly** 🚌 **7, 9, 11, 39**

Royal Barges National Museum

A collection of the king's ceremonial boats and barges, used each year at the end of the Buddhist Rains Retreat.

✉ **Bangkok Noi Canal, Thonburi side of Chao Phraya** ☎ **(02) 424 0004** 🕐 **Daily 9–4.**

Closed 31 Dec, 1 Jan, 12–14 Apr
🚌 **7, 9, 11**

Vimanmek Palace (➤ 38)

The largest golden teakwood building in the world, containing a superb collection of Ratanakosin period objects.

✉ **Thanon U-Thong Nai**
☎ **(02) 281 4715** 🕐 **Daily 9:30–3** 🚌 **10**

Chiang Mai
Wat Chiang Man

Built in 1296 by King Mengrai, the founder of Chiang Mai. The *viharn* contains two of the north's most sacred Buddha images.

✉ **Thanon Ratchaphakhinai**
🕐 **Daily 9–5**

National Museum

Fine collection of Buddha images in a variety of styles.

✉ **Superhighway 11, near Wat Jet Yot** 🕐 **Wed–Sun 9–4**

Tribal Museum

Dedicated to Thailand's hill people. Collections include handicrafts, jewellery, costumes and other items.

✉ **Ratchamangkhala Park, north of city** 🕐 **Mon–Fri 9–4**

Sukhothai
Ramkhamhaeng National Museum (➤ 25)

Excellent collection of Sukhothai–period objects. Probably the best place to start a visit to the ruins.

✉ **Sukhothai Historical Park**
🕐 **Daily 9–4**

Ubon Ratchathani
Ubon National Museum

Exhibits cover Isaan history, including prehistory. Museum building is a former palace.

✉ **Thanon Kheuan Thani**
🕐 **Daily 9–12, 1–4**

Nightlife

Bangkok

Bar Baska
Retro building given a Balinese feel. Very popular at weekends.
✉ 82–83 Ekamai Soi 22 ☎ (02) 711 4748/9 🕐 Daily 6PM–2AM
🚇 Ekamai 🚌 1, 8

Imageries By The Glass
Some of Bangkok's finest bands play here as well as the occasional foreign group. All types of modern music.
✉ 2 Sukhumvit Soi 24 ☎ (02) 261 6307 🕐 Mon–Thu 6–1:30, Fri–Sat 6PM–2AM 🚇 E5 Phrom Phong Station 🚌 1, 8, 11, 13, 38

La Luna
A big entertainment complex with a good disco and live music in the huge pub. Previously called Taurus.
✉ Sukhumvit Soi 26 ☎ (02) 261 3991 🕐 Daily 6PM–2AM
🚇 E5 Phrom Phong Station 🚌 1, 8, 11, 13, 38

Narcissus
One of Bangkok's most popular nightclubs.
✉ 111 Sukhumvit Soi 23 ☎ (02) 258 2549 🕐 Daily 9PM–2AM 🚇 Asoke 🚌 1, 8

Phuture
Large hi-tech disco popular with affluent young Thais and expatriates. Live music events occasionally.
✉ Chao Phraya Park Hotel, 91/9 Thanon Ratchadapisek ☎ (02) 693 8022 🕐 Daily 9PM–2AM 🚌 4, 10, 29

Saxophone Pub
An old established venue for live jazz; now blues and rock have been added.
✉ 3/8 Victory Monument, Thanon Phayathai ☎ (02) 246 5472 🕐 Daily 6PM–2AM

🚇 N3 Victory Monument Station 🚌 2, 3, 9, 10, 13

Chiang Mai

Bubbles Disco
An evergreen on the Chiang Mai night scene, popular with Thais and foreigners.
✉ Pornping Tower Hotel, 46–8 Thanon Charoen Prathet ☎ (053) 270099 🕐 Daily 9PM–2AM

Riverside
A large riverside bar and restaurant with two live bands nightly.
✉ 9/11 Thanon Charoen Rat ☎ (053) 243239 🕐 Daily 10PM–1:30AM

Ko Samui

Reggae Pub
A large open-air dance floor swings to the latest sounds as well as reggae.
✉ Chaweng Beach 🕐 Daily 10PM–2AM

Pattaya

Alcazar
The ultimate drag-queen show, complete with extravagant sets.
✉ 78/14 Thanon Pattaya 2 ☎ (038) 428746 🕐 Daily evening shows 6:30, 8 and 9:30 (and 11PM on Sat)

Pattaya Palladium
A large entertainment complex with reputedly the largest disco in Thailand.
✉ 78/33–35 Thanon Pattaya 2 ☎ (038) 424922 🕐 Daily 11AM–12 midnight

Phuket

Banana Discotheque
Dance club with an attached pub, popular with couples.
✉ 124 Thawiwong Road ☎ (076) 340301 🕐 Daily 9PM–2AM

Safety

Thailand's nightlife is legendary and, contrary to some uninformed opinion, does not just revolve around prostitution. Thais love nothing better than wining, dining and dancing. Particularly popular are the many *suan ahaan* or 'garden restaurants' in which Thais and foreign visitors, including children, can dine in garden settings, usually beside or on elegant platforms over lakes and ponds. Thailand is generally safe at night, although visitors should be discreet and not carry excessive amounts of cash. Generally speaking, Bangkok by night is safer than London, New York or Sydney.

Katoeys

Thai transvestites or *katoeys* ('lady boys') are very convincing – but despite their smooth skins and feminine attire, they often have a man's strength and a capacity for truculence. Watch for large hands and feet, Adam's apples and a precociousness of manner no Thai lady would ever exhibit. Spectacular transvestite stage shows have become a staple at tourist resorts such as Pattaya and Phuket.

Sports

Thai Boxing
Muay Thai or Thai boxing, also known as 'kick boxing', is enduringly popular in Thailand. Skilled, fast moving and entertaining, it is also a tough sport. In addition to gloved fists, the elbows, knees, feet and indeed any part of the body except the head can be used to strike one's opponent.

Bangkok
Amorn and Sons
Good tennis facilities and coaching, as well as squash and badminton courts.
✉ 8 Amorn Soi 3, Sukhumvit Soi 39 ☎ (02) 392 8442
🕐 7AM–10:30PM

Bike & Travel
Based in Pathum Thani, Bike & Travel offers cycling and canoe tours, including trips to Khao Yai National Park.
✉ 802/756 River Park, Moo 12, Thanon Phahon Yothin, Pathum Thani ☎ (02) 990 0274; e-mail: tanin@cyclingthailand.com

Kan Tarat Golf Course
Set between the runways of Bangkok International Airport and the military airport, this tight, 18-hole course sounds dangerous but is actually great fun.
✉ Don Muang Airport
☎ (02) 5343840

Kim Bowl
A new, state-of-the-art, 28-lane ten-pin bowling alley with karaoke rooms on site.
✉ Floor 7, MBK, 444 Thanon Phayathai ☎ (02) 611 7171
🕐 Sun–Thu 10AM–1AM, Fri–Sat 10AM–2AM 🚇 Ma Boon Krong
🚌 1, 2, 8

Lumpini Boxing Stadium
Here you can watch the world's top *Muay Thai* (Thai-style boxing) exponents. Bouts can be quite bloody.
✉ Thanon Rama IV, near Lumpini Park ☎ (02) 251 4303
🕐 Tue, Fri 6:30–11, Sat 5:30–8 and 8:30PM–midnight 🚌 7

Royal Bangkok Sports Club
Horse-racing on alternate Sundays; always a full card of races.
✉ 1 Thanon Henri Dunant
☎ (02) 251 0181 🕐 Sun 12:30–6 🚇 S1 Ratchadamri Station 🚌 4, 5

Royal Turf Club
A full card of races on the other Sunday to the Royal Bangkok Sports Club.
✉ 183 Thanon Phitsanulok
☎ (02) 280 0020
🕐 Sun 12:30–6 🚌 5, 9, 11

Chiang Mai
Chiang Mai Sky Adventure
Offers microlight flights giving unique views of the historic city of Chiang Mai. Trips last either 15 or 30 minutes and you are welcome to bring your camera along.
✉ 143 Moo 6, Chiang Doi, Amphur Doi Saket ☎ (053) 867646; fax (053) 868460; e-mail flying@cmnet.co.th

Gymkhana Club
The second oldest sports club in Southeast Asia houses squash and tennis courts, as well as a beautiful nine-hole golf course.
✉ Chiang Mai–Lamphun Road
☎ (053) 241035

Lanna Sports Club
A 27-hole golf course with tennis and badminton courts, horse riding and an excellent fitness centre.
✉ KM1 Thanon Chotana
☎ (053) 221911 🕐 Tee off 6

The Peak
Situated next door to Chiang Mai's famous Night Bazaar, The Peak offers visitors the chance to test their mountaineering skills on a man-made cliff.
✉ Night Market, Thanon Chang Klan ☎ (053) 800567-8
🕐 Daily 2–11

Thai Adventure Rafting

Two-day rafting adventures on the Pai River. The trips take in waterfalls, gorges and rapids.

✉ **73/7 Charoen Prathet (near the Diamond Riverside Hotel)** ☎ **(053) 277178; fax (053) 279505; e-mail: info@activethailand.com**

Velocity Cycle Hire and Tours

Chiang Mai's quiet roads leading off into the hills are perfect for keen cyclists. Bikes can be rented from this shop.

✉ **177 Thanon Changpuek, Sripoom** ☎ **(053) 410665; fax: (053) 410665**

Ko Samui
Big Game Fishing

Either go angling in the daytime off the coast of Ko Pha-Ngan or take a night boat and fish with the aid of spotlights. You can keep or sell what you haul in.

✉ **AK Travel, 20/5 Moo 1, Choeng Mon Beach** ☎ **(077) 425390; e-mail aktravel-@samart.co.th**

Samui Sports Divers

A highly professional dive company that takes pleasure in getting the most out of any prospective diver. There are trips to nearby islands for the casual snorkeller.

✉ **Bo Phut Village** ☎ **(077) 427204; fax (077) 427203; e-mail: info@samuisportsdivers.com**

Krabi
Ao Nang Muay Thai

View Thailand's national sport, *Muay Thai* (Thai-style boxing), at the beach.

✉ **Ao Nang Stadium, Ao Nang Beach** 🕐 **Sat 8pm–1am**

Phuket
Andaman Hooker Sport Fishing Charter

Phuket is a great place to go big-game fishing, with an abundance of marlin, sailfish and tuna in the waters. Andaman Hooker offers day trips or charter trips of up to five days.

✉ **6/6 Soi Suki Moo 9, Chalong Bay** ☎ **(076) 282036; fax (076) 282036; e-mail andamanhooker@phuket.com**

Ao Chalong Yacht Club

The club holds monthly yacht races and visitors to Phuket are welcome to join in.

✉ **Chalong Bay** ☎ **(076) 381914; fax: (076) 381934**

Phuket Country Club

A magnificent 27-hole golf course with a driving range. Visitors are welcome.

✉ **80/1 Vichitsongkram Road, Kathu** ☎ **(076) 321039; fax: (076) 321721**

Scuba Cat Diving

Trips to the Similan and Surin islands, where it is occasionally possible to glimpse the world's largest fish, the whale shark, as well as other sea creatures.

✉ **Patong Beach Road, Patong or Kata Beach (Kata main road)** ☎ **(076) 293120/1; fax (076) 293122; e-mail fly@scuba-cat.com**

Sea Canoe Thailand

Offers tours around scenic Phang-nga Bay in inflatable canoes, giving access to the bay's caves, something that is impossible with ordinary boats.

✉ **367/4 Yaowarat Road** ☎ **(076) 212252; fax: (076) 212172**

Television

Thai domestic television offers six channels of mixed quality, including some English-language broadcasts and, on many films, a dual soundtrack – the original English is available on FM radio. Cable TV (UBC) is now widely available, with BBC, CNN and a range of movie channels.

What's On When

Loy Krathong
Perhaps the most beautiful of all Thailand's festivals is Loy Krathong, where arrangements of flowers set with candles, incense and a small coin are floated on the waters (river, lake or sea). This custom is officially traced back to Nang Noppamat, a favourite queen of King Ramkhamhaeng, the great 13th-century ruler of Sukhothai, the first independent Thai kingdom. Nang Noppamat first floated a *krathong* for her king and Thais have been floating them in their millions ever since.

Thailand has many festivals and temple fairs, especially between November and February. Dates for festivals vary from year to year, either due to the lunar calendar or because the local authorities decide to change dates.

Chinese New Year in January or February is not a public holiday, but most shops close.

January
Don Chedi Monument Fair, Suphanburi: commemorates King Naresuan's victory over Burmese invaders in 1592.
That Phanom Festival, That Phanom: week-long festival paying homage to Wat Phra That Phanom.

February
Flower Festival, Chiang Mai: includes a lively parade.
Phra Nakhon Khiri Diamond Festival, Phetchaburi: celebrates local history.
Chinese New Year, Nakhon Sawan: Chinese New Year festivities are at their most exuberant.

March
ASEAN Barred Ground Dove Fair, Yala: dove-cooing contest featuring contestants from Southeast Asia.
International Jewellery Fair, Bangkok: features buyers and sellers from around the world.
Phanom Rung Festival, Phanom Rung: light shows and processions celebrate the history of this Khmer temple.
Phra Phutthabaat Festival, Saraburi: pilgrimage to Wat Phra Phutthabaat.

Mid-May to mid-June
Bun Prawet Festival, Loei (Dan Sai district): animist-Buddhist celebration with wild masks and costumes.
Rocket Festival, Yasothon (and all over the northeast): huge, home-made rockets are launched to bring rain to the rice fields.
Royal Ploughing Ceremony, Bangkok: ancient Brahman ritual held at Sanam Luang.

July
Candle Festival, Ubon Ratchathani (and all over the northeast): candles parade.

September
International Swan-Boat Races, Bangkok: on the Chao Phraya River.
Narathiwat Fair, Narathiwat: a week celebrating southern culture.

Late September to early October
Vegetarian Festival, Phuket: nine days of feasting plus acts of self-mortification to the nine emperor gods of Taoism.

November
Loy Krathong, whole country (best in the north and Sukhothai): on full-moon night, small lotus-shaped baskets with flowers and candles are floated on rivers, lakes and canals.
Elephant Roundup, Surin: elephants play football, re-enact battles and roll logs, among other feats.

Late November to early December
River Kwai Bridge Week, Kanchanaburi: includes nightly sound-and-light shows.

Practical Matters

Above: a line of
tuk-tuks *waits for
custom in Bangkok*
Right: *the red,
white and blue
stripes of the
Thai flag flutter
in the breeze*

117

GMT 12 noon	Thailand 7PM	Germany 1PM	USA (NY) 7AM	Netherlands 1PM	Spain 1PM

BEFORE YOU GO

WHAT YOU NEED

	UK	Germany	USA	Netherlands	Spain
Passport (must be valid for 6 months beyond period of stay)	●	●	●	●	●
Visa (regulations can change – check before your journey)	●	●	●	●	●
Onward or Return Ticket	○	○	○	○	○
Health Inoculations	○	○	○	○	○
Health Documentation (➤ 123, Health)	○	○	○	○	○
Travel Insurance	○	○	○	○	○
Driving Licence (international)	●	●	●	●	●
Car Insurance Certificate (included if car is rented)	▲	▲	▲	▲	▲
Car Registration Document (included if car is rented)	▲	▲	▲	▲	▲

● Required ○ Suggested ▲ Not required

Some countries require a passport to remain valid for a minimum period (usually at least six months) beyond the date of entry – contact their consulate or embassy or your travel agent for details.

WHEN TO GO

Bangkok

High season

Low season

JAN	FEB	MAR	APR	MAY	JUN	JUL	AUG	SEP	OCT	NOV	DEC
29°C	31°C	33°C	35°C	34°C	32°C	31°C	31°C	31°C	30°C	30°C	29°C
☀	☀	☀	☀	🌧	🌧	🌧	🌧	🌧	🌧	☀	☀

☀ Sun   🌧 Wet

TOURIST OFFICES

In the UK
Tourism Authority of Thailand
✉ 3rd Floor, Brook House, 98–99 Jermyn Street, London SW1Y 6EE
☎ (020) 7925 2511
Fax: (020) 7925 2512

In the USA
Tourism Authority of Thailand
✉ 61 Broadway, Suite 2810, New York NY 10006
☎ (212) 432 0433
Fax: (212) 269 25880

POLICE 191, 193

TOURIST POLICE 1155

FIRE 199

AMBULANCE 191

WHEN YOU ARE THERE

ARRIVING

Most visitors arrive by air through Bangkok International Airport. Bangkok is a regional hub for international air traffic and is served by more than 40 airlines. Smaller international airports are in Chiang Mai and Phuket. Thai Airways is the national carrier ☎ (02) 545 3889.

Bangkok Int. Airport Distance to city centre	Journey times
25 kilometres	🚌 50 minutes
	🚐 80 minutes
	🚗 30 minutes

Chiang Mai Airport Distance to city centre	Journey times
4 kilometres	🚌 N/A
	🚐 N/A
	🚗 10 minutes

MONEY

Thai currency is decimal based and divided into baht and satang. There are 100 satang to 1 baht. Coins now in circulation are in denominations of 25 and 50 satang and in 1, 5 and 10 baht. Notes are in denominations of 10, 20, 50, 100, 500 and 1000 baht.

Credit cards including Visa, MasterCard, American Express and Diner's Club are accepted at all luxury hotels and the more expensive restaurants. Traveller's cheques can be cashed at banks and exchange counters in major towns and resorts.

TIME

 Thailand is 7 hours ahead of Greenwich Mean Time (GMT+7). Thailand's position within the tropical zone means that the number of daylight hours varies little over a year.

CUSTOMS

YES
There are specific allowances for the import of alcohol, cigarettes and luxury goods for those over 18 years of age:
Alcohol:
spirits: 1 litre
wine: 1 litre
Tobacco:
Cigarettes: 200 grams
Cigars: 250 grams
Tobacco: 250 grams
A limit of 50,000 baht applies on the import or export of Thai currency.
Inbound visitors are issued with two sets of papers to fill in: a customs declaration form, which must be handed over to the customs official on arrival, and a visa information form.

NO
Non-prescription drugs, pornography, firearms, certain fruits and vegetables. Antiques and Buddha images are not allowed to leave without proper permission from the relevant authorities.

TOURIST OFFICES

- Tourism Authority of
  Thailand (TAT) Head
  Office
  1600 New Petchburi Road
  Makkasan
  Ratchathewi
  Bangkok 10400
  ☎ (02) 250 5500
  Fax: (02) 250 5511

Local Offices
Bangkok
- 4 Thanon Ratchadamnoen
  Nok
  ☎ (02) 2282 9773

Chiang Mai
- 105/1 Chiang Mai-Lamphun
  Road
  ☎ (053) 248604

Chiang Rai
- Thanon Singkhlai
  ☎ (053) 717433

Pattaya
- 382/1 Thanon Chaihat,
  Pattaya City
  ☎ (038) 427667

Phuket
- 73–75 Phuket Road
  ☎ (076) 211036

The Tourism Authority of
Thailand (TAT) is a
government-run tourist
information service providing
excellent pamphlets on travel
and tourism. With more than
20 offices around the country
and 16 overseas branches,
the TAT is in a position to
regulate all tourism-related
businesses, cutting out most
unscrupulous operators.

NATIONAL HOLIDAYS

J	F	M	A	M	J	J	A	S	O	N	D
1	1		2	3		1	1		1		3

1 Jan	New Year's Day
Feb	Magha Puja
6 Apr	Chakri Day
13–15 Apr	Songkran
1 May	Labour Day
5 May	Coronation Day
May	Visakha Puja
July	Asanha Puja
12 Aug	Queen's Birthday
23 Oct	King Chulalongkorn Day
5 Dec	King's Birthday
10 Dec	Constitution Day
31 Dec	New Year's Eve

Certain national holidays vary from year to year due
to them being fixed by the lunar calendar. Most shops
and department stores are open during national
holidays.

OPENING HOURS

○ Shops	● Attractions/museums
● Offices	○ Post offices
● Banks	○ Pharmacies

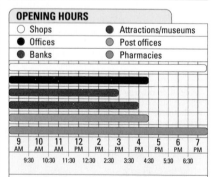

9 AM	10 AM	11 AM	12 PM	2 PM	3 PM	4 PM	5 PM	6 PM	7 PM
9:30	10:30	11:30	12:30	2:30	3:30	4:30	5:30	6:30	

In the larger cities some pharmacies stay open 24
hours. Small shops are usually open by 8:30AM and
tend to close by 6PM. Department stores open about
10AM and close as late as 10PM. Markets open as
early as 3AM and many are finished by 8AM; others
stay open until the early afternoon. National
museums normally follow the times stated above,
but the many privately run museums vary. All
government offices, post offices and banks close
for national holidays.

PUBLIC TRANSPORT

 Internal Flights Thai Airways (THAI), Bangkok Airways and newcomer Phuket Airways link all the major towns and cities within the country, flying to more than 25 destinations. Occasionally THAI offers special domestic air passes with quite reasonable savings. These need to be purchased outside the country.

 Trains Thailand's domestic rail network, run by the State Railway of Thailand (SRT), serves most major towns. Journey times are quite long due the narrowness of the gauge. Nevertheless trains are comfortable and overnight journeys include your own bed. The train remains a cheap and safe way to travel in Thailand. Bookings should be made at Bangkok's Hualamphong Station ☎ (02) 223 3762.

 Bus Travel Thailand has a variety of government and privately run bus services. To reach certain places your only option may be the orange, non-air-conditioned government buses. These take a long time to reach their destination, stopping at every village en route. A better option is to take the faster government or privately run air-conditioned buses that rarely stop. Drinks and snacks are included in the price of the ticket.

 Urban Transport Bangkok has a new mass transit system, the Skytrain. Journeys which used to take hours now take minutes. Three routes serve most of Bangkok's important destinations. Bangkok's bus system is extensive and air-conditioned buses go just about everywhere. Bus services in other towns around the country are rudimentary; Chiang Mai no longer has a bus service. Smaller buses called *songthaews* serve most towns.

CAR RENTAL

It is possible to rent vehicles in all major tourist destinations. The large international rental companies have offices in the country, as do many smaller, local rental companies. A four-wheel drive, with its off-road access, is best in the north.

TAXIS

 Taxis cruise all Bangkok's major streets. Be careful that the meter is switched on at the beginning of a journey. Fares are very reasonable, therefore a small tip is expected. Only a very few taxis operate in other parts of the country.

DRIVING

 Speed limit on expressways: **120kph**

Speed limit on main roads: **100kph**

Speed limit on urban roads: **50kph**

 Seat belts must be worn in front seats at all times.

 Random breath-testing. Never drive under the influence of alcohol.

 Petrol comes in unleaded 95 octane and unleaded 91 octane. Diesel is also available. All are sold by the litre. Service stations abound in all the larger towns and cities but be careful to fill up for longer, cross-country journeys.

 There are plenty of motor repair garages throughout the country. Most service stations will also be able to offer some help in the event of a breakdown. International car rental companies include a free breakdown service in their rental packages. Most local rental companies also provide a breakdown service but charge extra.

PERSONAL SAFETY

Generally Thailand is a safe country for visitors. Amazingly, considering its wild nightlife, Bangkok is one of the safest capital cities in the world. However, certain precautions should be taken to ensure personal safety:

- If trekking or rafting take good maps, dress sensibly and leave an itinerary of your journey with someone.
- Dress conservatively; avoid wearing revealing clothes.
- Beware of petty thieves on long-distance buses.
- Avoid unofficial taxis if arriving at Bangkok airport at night.

Police assistance:
☎ 191, 193
from any call box

TELEPHONES

International calls can be made from most hotels. International phones can also be found in most of Thailand's airports and there are a few international call boxes in shopping malls. Some payphones are coin operated and others use cards, which can be purchased at newsagents, shops and post offices.

International Dialling Codes

From Thailand dial 001 then:	
UK	44
Germany	49
USA	1
Netherlands	31
Spain	34

POST

The Thai postal service is very efficient. Postal rates within the country are low and international rates also very reasonable. To register an item there is an extra charge of 25 baht. Every town has a post office selling stamps and stationery.

ELECTRICITY

The power supply is: 220 volts, 50 cycles AC.
Plug sockets are usually two

flat-pronged terminals or two round-pole terminals.

Adaptors can be purchased at any electrical store for all international plug types.

TIPS/GRATUITIES

Yes ✓ No ✗		
Restaurants (VAT and service charge)	✓	
Tour guides	✓	
Hairdressers	✗	
Taxi drivers	✓	
Chambermaids	✗	
Porters	✓	
Toilets	✗	

PHOTOGRAPHY

What to photograph: Temples, mountains, hill tribes, festivals, markets, rural life, canal and river life.
Best time to photograph: The weather is sunny and clear between November and March, although photography is possible all year round.
Where to buy film: Film and batteries of all types are readily available from shops and airports. Processing facilities are good.

HEALTH

Insurance
All visitors are strongly recommended to arrange medical insurance before leaving for Thailand; this should include home transport. Medical facilities are good.

Dental Services
Dental clinics are of a high standard and all major tourist destinations have plenty to choose from.

Sun Advice
The sun in Thailand is extremely powerful and sun protection is essential. A sun hat should be mandatory on long walks, especially during the midday hours. Sun cream with a high protection factor is also necessary. Ensure children are properly protected.

Drugs
Most chemists in Thailand speak English and pharmacies stay open long hours. Most Western medicine is available but if you are on special or unusual medication, remember to bring supplies with you as there is no guarantee that they will be on sale locally.

Safe Water
Although city water supplies are chlorinated, avoid drinking tap water. Bottled drinking water is provided in restaurants and can be bought from shops and service stations everywhere in the country.

CONCESSIONS

Students/Youths Certain museums and guest houses offer reduced rates for holders of International Student Identity Cards. These cards are available from the International Student Travel Confederation based in Denmark.

✉ Box 9048, DK1000, Copenhagen, Denmark
☎ 3393 9303; fax: 3393 7377

Senior Citizens There are almost no concessions for the older visitor. However, this is more than made up for by the way in which the Thais treat older people. Age implies status and respect.

CLOTHING SIZES

Thailand	UK	Europe	USA	
46	36	46	36	Suits
48	38	48	38	Suits
50	40	50	40	Suits
52	42	52	42	Suits
54	44	54	44	Suits
56	46	56	46	Suits
41	7	41	8	Shoes
42	7.5	42	8.5	Shoes
43	8.5	43	9.5	Shoes
44	9.5	44	10.5	Shoes
45	10.5	45	11.5	Shoes
46	11	46	12	Shoes
37	14.5	37	14.5	Shirts
38	15	38	15	Shirts
39/40	15.5	39/40	15.5	Shirts
41	16	41	16	Shirts
42	16.5	42	16.5	Shirts
43	17	43	17	Shirts
34	8	34	6	Dresses
36	10	36	8	Dresses
38	12	38	10	Dresses
40	14	40	12	Dresses
42	16	42	14	Dresses
44	18	44	16	Dresses
4.5	4.5	37.5	6	Shoes
38	5	38	6.5	Shoes
38.5	5.5	38.5	7	Shoes
39	6	39	7.5	Shoes
40	6.5	40	8	Shoes
41	7	41	8.5	Shoes

LANGUAGE

Thailand's official language is Thai, although there are considerable regional variations in the north, northeast and south.

Thai is a tonal language related to Chinese, with a complex script derived from Sanskrit. It is not easy to learn and very few foreigners acquire any degree of fluency. However, English is widely spoken and Thais everywhere will welcome and sympathise with your halting attempts at speaking their language.

General phrases/words

hello/goodbye	sawàt-dii khráp (man) sawàt-dii khâ (woman)	inexpensive	thùuk
		no	mâi châi
hotel	rohng raem	thank you	khàwp khun
how are you?	sàbaai dii, mǎi?	toilet	hâwng sûam
how much is this?	níi thâo rai?	too expensive	phaeng pai
		well, thank you	sàbaai dii, khàwp khun
I don't under-stand	mâi khâo jai	where is the . . ?	yùu thîî nǎi?
I would like to go to . . .	yàak jà pai...	yes	châi

Days

Monday	wan jan	Friday	wan sùk
Tuesday	wan angkhaan	Saturday	wan sǎo
Wednesday	wan phút	Sunday	wan aathít
Thursday	wan phréuhàt		

Food and drink

beef	néua	pork	muu
chicken	gài	rice	khâo
coffee	kafae	shrimp	kûng
fish	plaa	tea	chaa
fried rice	khâo phàt	vegetables	phàk
fruit	phǒn-lá-mái	water	náam plào
noodles	kuay tiaw		

Numbers

one	nèung	nine	kâo
two	sǎwng	10	sip
three	sǎam	20	yîi-sip
four	sìi	30	sǎam-sip
five	hâa	100	nèung ráwy
six	hòk	1,000	nèung phan
seven	jèt		
eight	pàet		

INDEX

Acknowledgements
The Automobile Association wishes to thank the following photographers and libraries for their assistance in the preparation of this book.
CPA/David Henley 87, 90.

All remaining images are held in the Association's own library (AA World Travel Library) with contributions from the following photographers:
Ben Davies 21c, 75c; David Henley 5b, 6c, 9c, 14c, 15t, 16t, 16c, 17t, 17b, 18t, 19tr, 20t, 21t, 22t, 22b, 23t, 24t, 24c, 25t, 25b, 26t, 26c, 26b, 30, 32t, 48/8, 52b, 53c, 55, 56, 57t, 60t, 60c, 63, 67, 68t, 71t, 72t, 73t, 74t, 75t, 76t, 77t, 78t, 79t, 80t, 80cl, 81b, 122t, 122l, 122r; Jim Holmes 33r, 91t, 92, 93, 94, 95, 96, 97, 98, 99, 100, 101, 102, 013, 104, 105, 106, 107, 108, 109, 110, 111, 112, 113, 114, 115, 116; R Strange 1, 2, 5t, 6t, 7t, 7c, 8t, 8c, 8b, 9t, 9b, 10t, 10b, 11t, 11c, 12t, 12tl, 12c, 12b, 13t, 13l, 13b, 14t, 15b, 18cl, 18/19, 19tl, 19cr, 20b, 23b, 27t, 27b, 28t, 29t, 31, 32l, 33t, 34t, 35t, 36t, 37t, 37b, 38b, 39t, 39b, 40t, 41t, 43t, 43r, 45, 46, 47tr, 47t, 48cl, 48bl, 49tr, 49t, 50t, 50b, 51t, 51b, 52t, 53t, 53b, 57c, 59tl, 59tr, 61, 62, 64, 65, 66, 68bl, 69t, 69br, 70, 71b, 72cl, 72c, 73c, 74cl, 76b, 77c, 78r, 79b, 80c, 80b, 81t, 81c, 82, 83, 84, 85, 86t, 86b, 87t, 88, 89t, 91b, 117t, 117b.

Dear Essential Traveller

Your comments, opinions and recommendations are very important to us. So please help us to improve our travel guides by taking a few minutes to complete this simple questionnaire.

You do not need a stamp (unless posted outside the UK). If you do not want to cut this page from your guide, then photocopy it or write your answers on a plain sheet of paper.

Send to: **The Editor, AA World Travel Guides, FREEPOST SCE 4598, Basingstoke RG21 4GY.**

Your recommendations…

We always encourage readers' recommendations for restaurants, nightlife or shopping – if your recommendation is used in the next edition of the guide, we will send you a *FREE* AA *Essential* **Guide** of your choice. Please state below the establishment name, location and your reasons for recommending it.

_____

_____

_____

_____

Please send me **AA *Essential*** _____

About this guide…

Which title did you buy?

    AA *Essential* _____

Where did you buy it? _____

When? m̲ m̲ / y̲ y̲

Why did you choose an AA *Essential* Guide? _____

_____

_____

_____

_____

Did this guide meet your expectations?

    Exceeded ☐ Met all ☐ Met most ☐ Fell below ☐

    Please give your reasons _____

_____

_____

_____

continued on next page…

Were there any aspects of this guide that you particularly liked? _____
_____
_____

Is there anything we could have done better? _____
_____
_____

About you...

Name (*Mr/Mrs/Ms*) _____
    Address _____
_____
_____ Postcode _____
    Daytime tel nos _____

Please only give us your mobile phone number if you wish to hear from us
about other products and services from the AA and partners by text or mms.

Which age group are you in?
    Under 25 ☐ 25–34 ☐ 35–44 ☐ 45–54 ☐ 55–64 ☐ 65+ ☐

How many trips do you make a year?
    Less than one ☐ One ☐ Two ☐ Three or more ☐

Are you an AA member? Yes ☐ No ☐

About your trip...

When did you book? m m / y y   When did you travel? m m / y y
How long did you stay? _____
Was it for business or leisure? _____
Did you buy any other travel guides for your trip?
    If yes, which ones? _____

Happy Holidays!

ATLAS SYMBOLS

English	French / Dutch
Highway, multilane divided road - under construction / Autobahn, mehrspurige Straße - in Bau	Autoroute, route à plusieurs voies - en construction / Autosnelweg, weg met meer rijstroken - in aanleg
Trunk road - under construction / Fernverkehrsstraße - in Bau	Route à grande circulation - en construction / Weg voor interlokaal verkeer - in aanleg
Principal highway / Hauptstraße	Route principale / Hoofdweg
Secondary road / Nebenstraße	Route secondaire / Overige verharde wegen
Practicable road, track / Fahrweg, Piste	Chemin carrossable, piste / Weg, piste
Road numbering / Straßennummerierung — 24	Numérotage des routes / Wegnummering
Distances in kilometres / Entfernungen in Kilometer — **259** 130 129	Distances en kilomètres / Afstand in kilometers
Height in meters - Pass / Höhe in Meter - Pass — 1365	Altitude en mètres - Col / Hoogte in meters - Pas
Railway - Railway ferry / Eisenbahn - Eisenbahnfähre	Chemin-de-fer - Ferry-boat / Spoorweg - Spoorpont
Car ferry - Shipping route / Autofähre - Schifffahrtslinie	Bac autos - Ligne maritime / Autoveer - Scheepvaartlijn
Major international airport - Airport / Wichtiger internationaler Flughafen - Flughafen ✈ ✈	Aéroport importante international - Aéroport / Belangrijke internationale luchthaven - Luchthaven
International boundary - Province boundary / Internationale Grenze - Provinzgrenze	Frontière internationale - Limite de Province / Internationale grens - Provinciale grens
Undefined boundary / Unbestimmte Grenze	Frontière d'Etat non définie / Rijksgrens onbepaalt
Time zone boundary / Zeitzonengrenze — -4h Greenwich Time / -3h Greenwich Time	Limite de fuseau horaire / Tijdzone-grens
National capital / Hauptstadt eines souveränen Staates — **BANGKOK**	Capitale nationale / Hoofdstad van een souvereine staat
Federal capital / Hauptstadt eines Bundesstaates — **Tak**	Capitale d'un état fédéral / Hoofdstad van een deelstaat
Restricted area / Sperrgebiet	Zone interdite / Verboden gebied
National park / Nationalpark	Parc national / Nationaal park
Ancient monument / Antikes Baudenkmal	Monuments antiques / Antiek monument
Interesting cultural monument / Sehenswertes Kulturdenkmal — *Angkor Wat* ✱	Monument culturel intéressant / Bezienswaardig cultuurmonument
Interesting natural monument / Sehenswertes Naturdenkmal — *Ha Long Bay* ✱	Monument naturel intéressant / Bezienswaardig natuurmonument
Well / Brunnen	Puits / Bron

0 — 100 km
0 — 60 miles

Maps © Mairs Geographischer Verlag / Falk Verlag, 73751 Ostfildern

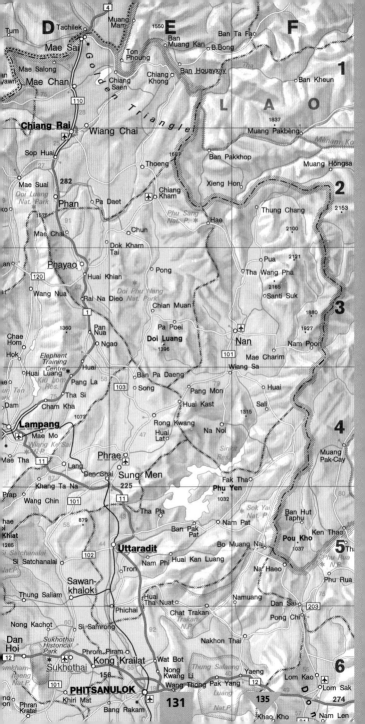

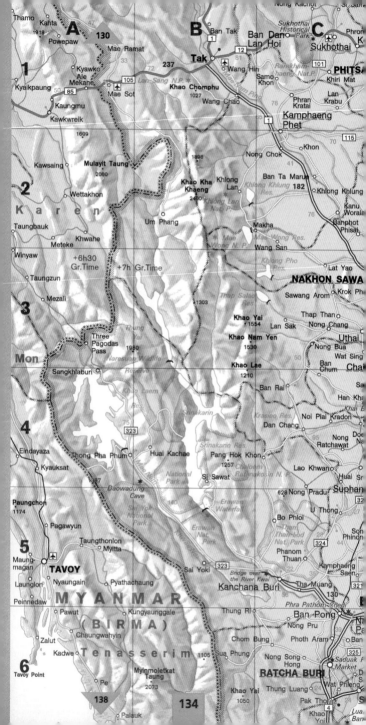

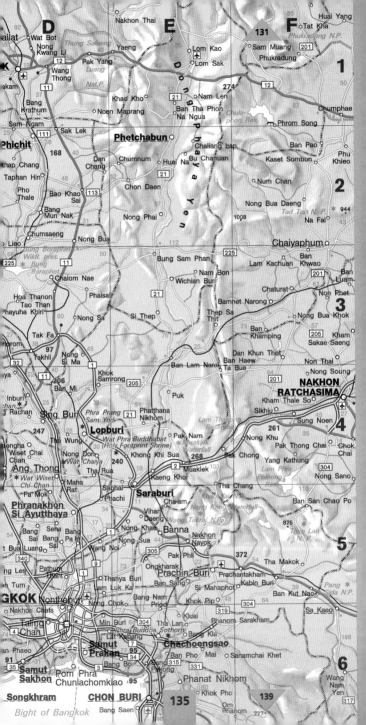

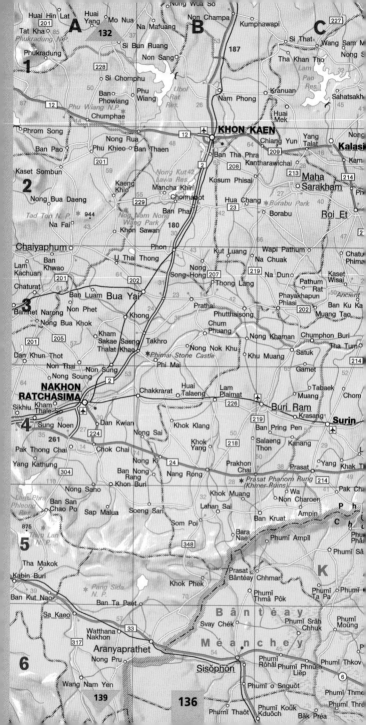

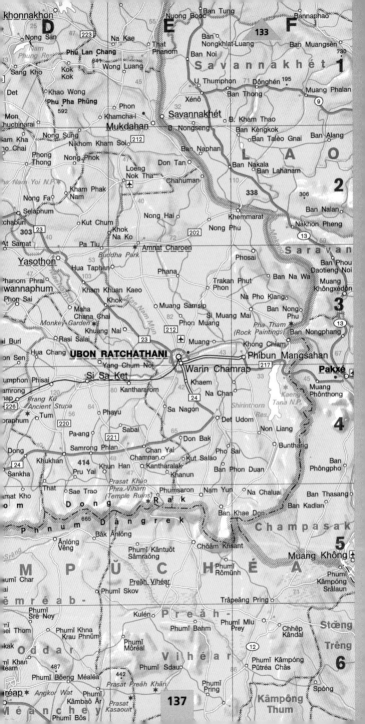

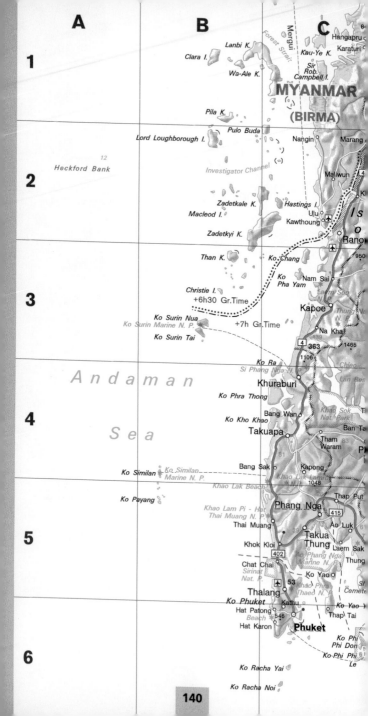

Grid references (columns A–C, rows 1–6)

Column B / Row 1
- Clara I.
- Lanbi K.
- Wa-Ale K.
- Mergui
- Forest Strait

Column C / Row 1
- Hangapru
- Kau-Ye K.
- Karaturi
- Sir Rob. Campbell I.
- MYANMAR (BIRMA)

Row 2
- Pila K.
- Pulo Buda
- Lord Loughborough I.
- Nangin
- Marang
- Heckford Bank
- 12
- Investigator Channel
- Maliwun
- 4
- K

Row 2/3
- Zadetkale K.
- Macleod I.
- Hastings I.
- Ulu
- Kawthoung
- Zadetkyi K.
- Is
- o
- Rano

Row 3
- Than K.
- Ko Chang
- 950
- Ko Pha Yam
- Nam Sai
- Christie I.
- +6h30 Gr.Time
- Laem Son N. P.
- Kapoe
- Thung N. P.
- Ko Surin Nua
- Ko Surin Marine N. P.
- +7h Gr.Time
- Na Khai
- Ko Surin Tai
- 4 363
- 1465
- 1106
- Chieo

Row 4
- A n d a m a n
- Ko Ra
- Si Phang Nga N.
- Lan Res
- Khuraburi
- Ko Phra Thong
- S e a
- Bang Wan
- Khao Sok Nat. Park
- Ko Kho Khao
- Ban Ta
- Takuapa
- Tham Waram
- P
- 81

Row 4/5
- Bang Sak
- Kapong
- Ko Similan
- Ko Similan Marine N. P.
- Khao Lak - Lamru N. P.
- 1048
- Khao Lak Beach
- Ko Payang
- Thap Put
- Khao Lam Pi - Hat Thai Muang N. P.
- Phang Nga
- Thai Muang
- 415
- Ao Luk

Row 5
- Khok Kloi
- Takua Thung
- Laem Sak
- 402
- Ao Phang Nga Marine N.
- Thung
- Chat Chai
- Ko Yao
- Sirinat Nat. P.
- Ko Yao
- Thalang
- 53
- Khao Phra Thaeo N. P.
- Cemete
- Ko Phuket
- Kathu
- Si

Row 5/6
- Hat Patong Beach
- 546
- Ko Yao
- Hat Karon
- Thap Tai
- Phuket
- Ko Phi Phi Don
- Ko-Phi Phi Le

Row 6
- Ko Racha Yai
- Ko Racha Noi

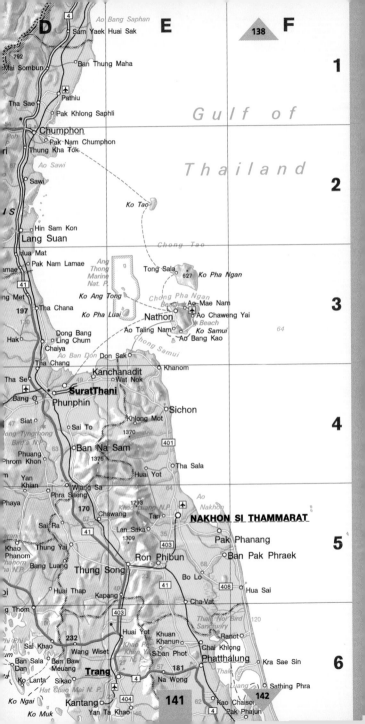

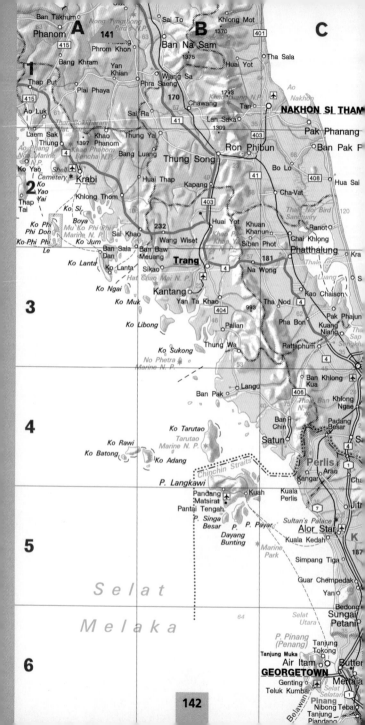

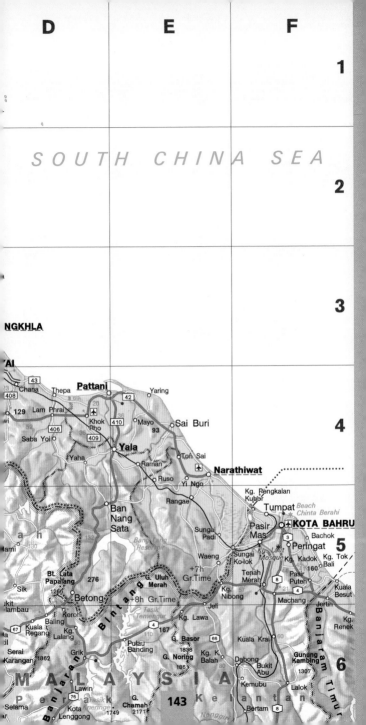

D E F

1

SOUTH CHINA SEA

2

3

NGKHLA

AI

43 Chana Thepa   **Pattani**   Yaring

408 129 Lam Phrai 42
Khok 410 Mayo
Rho 93   **Sai Buri**
406
Saba Yoi 409   **Yala**
Yaha   Raman   Ton Sai
Ruso   **Narathiwat**
Yi Ngo

4

Kg. Pengkalan
Kubor
Rangae   **Tumpat** *Beach*
Chinta Berahi
Ban   **Pasir**   **KOTA BAHRU**
Nang   Sungai **Mas**   *Kg. Laut* 3 **Peringat**
Sata   Padi   Sungai *Mosque* Kg. Kadok Kg. Tok
Bang Lang   Ko-lok   Pasir 160 Bali
Reservoir   Waeng   Tenah Puteh 8 Kuala
+7h   Merah 4 Besut
Bt. Lata 276   Gr.Time   Kg. Machang Jertih
Papalang   **G. Uluh**   Nibong   Kg.
1266   **Merah**   Kg. Lawa   Renek
Sik   **Betong** +8h Gr.Time   Jeli
Tasik
Temengur
Keroh   **G. Basor** 66   Kuala Krai 60 **Gunung**
Kuala Baling   110 167 1838   **Kambing**
Regang Kg.   Pulau **G. Noring** Kg. K.   Dabong 1307
Lalang   Banding 186   Balah   Bukit
Serai   Grik   Abu
Karangan 1862   Kemubu   Bertam 8
Lalok

5

6

M A L A Y S I A
Lawin   *Banjaran*   **143**   *K e l a n t a n*
Selama 76 amsik **G.**   *Banjaran Timur*
Kota *neringei* **Chamah**
Lenggong 1749 2171   Nenggiri

Sight Locator Index

This index relates to the atlas section on pages 130–143. We have given map references to the main sights of interest in the book. Some sights in the index may not be plotted on the atlas. Note: ibc – inside back cover

For the main index see pages 125–126